Mentor-Lernhilfe
Band 94

Nobody is perfect ...

Typische Fehler bei englischen Abschlußprüfungen

Von Hannelore Nuffer und Frank Steele

Mentor Verlag München

Hannelore Nuffer, Lehrerin am staatlich anerkannten Sprachen- und Dolmetscher-Institut München (Berufsfachschule und Fachakademie) sowie Dozentin an der Volkshochschule.

Frank Steele, B. A., Sprachlehrer, Dozent und Industrial Trainer, ehem. Lehrer in USA und hauptamtlicher pädagogischer Mitarbeiter an der Volkshochschule München, Autor und „educational consultant“ für verschiedene Verlage und Zeitschriften.

Acknowledgements

We are grateful to the following for permission to reproduce copyright material:
The Executors of the Estate of W. Somerset Maugham for the part of the story “The Lion’s Skin” by W. Somerset Maugham from “The Complete Short Stories” published by Heinemann Limited 1951, © by A. P. Watt Ltd, London; Ned Brown associated, Beverly Hills, for a paragraph from “Tales of Power” by Carlos Castaneda, published by Hodder and Stoughton Limited in 1975.

Photo auf S. 152: „Kinder bringen einer Katze das Lesen bei“ von Jan Steen mit freundlicher Genehmigung der „Öffentlichen Kunstsammlung, Kunstmuseum Basel“.

 Eselsbrücke

✗ Falsches Englisch

! Achtung!

Illustrationen von Jan Hoyer

Auflage: 6. 5. 4. 3. 2. | Letzte Zahlen
Jahr: 1990 89 88 87 86 | maßgeblich

Druck: Druckhaus Langenscheidt, Berlin
Printed in Germany. ISBN 3-580-64940-X

Vorwort

Nobody is perfect. Auch der Fortgeschrittene hat noch mit Problemen der englischen Sprache zu kämpfen. Er macht zwar immer weniger Fehler, aber manche sind hartnäckig, und gerade gegen diese wollen wir in diesem Buch angehen.
Ob Ihnen ein Prüfungstext liegt oder nicht, ob Sie jede Einzelheit verstehen oder nicht, haben Sie meist nicht in der Hand. Aber **wie** Sie sich sprachlich einwandfrei dazu äußern — und darum geht es doch vor allem — das können Sie lernen. Daß Sie dabei Ihre Fehler auf ein Minimum reduzieren, daß Ihre Formulierungen grammatikalisch richtig sind und wortschatzmäßig ins Schwarze treffen — dazu möchten wir Ihnen verhelfen. Wir konzentrieren uns dabei auf bestimmte Fehler, auf die wir bei Korrekturen von Prüfungsarbeiten immer wieder gestoßen sind. Natürlich konnten wir im Rahmen einer solchen Lernhilfe nicht auf alle Fehlerquellen eingehen. Aber wenn Sie die von uns behandelten Fehler **nicht** mehr machen, haben Sie schon viel gewonnen.
Sie werden beim Durchblättern feststellen, daß die einzelnen Kapitel sehr unterschiedlich aussehen. Sie lassen sich in folgende drei Gruppen einordnen:

— Kapitel, die vor allem auf Wortschatzprobleme eingehen (z.B. „Confounded Words“, „False Friends“)
— Kapitel, die vorwiegend Grammatikfehler behandeln (z.B. „Tenses“, „Adverbs“ etc.)
— Kapitel, die sich mit bestimmten Themen befassen und den dazugehörigen Redewendungen (z.B. „Crime and Punishment“, „An American Education“ etc.)

Die Probleme der Textanalyse konnten wir nur streifen.

Unser Vorschlag, wie Sie das Buch verwenden sollten: Lesen Sie jeweils einen Abschnitt durch.
Lassen Sie sich nicht durch einzelne Wörter, die Sie vielleicht nicht kennen, davon abhalten weiterzulesen, sondern versuchen Sie erst einmal zu verstehen, worum es im großen und ganzen geht. Das wird Ihnen bei manchen Kapiteln sehr leicht fallen, weil Ihnen der Inhalt schon vertraut ist. Dann gehen Sie gleich zu den Übungen über. Hier können Sie testen, ob Sie auch wirklich in der Lage sind, das Gelesene aktiv anzuwenden, und darum geht es doch eigentlich.
Manche Kapitel werden Ihnen schwerer fallen, dann lesen Sie die Erklärungen ein zweites Mal, nun am besten mit einem Rotstift. Unterstreichen Sie unbekannte Wörter und schlagen Sie sie nach. Wenn die Erläuterungen klar sind, können Sie sich an die Übungen machen, die Sie grundsätzlich erst einmal ganz durcharbeiten sollten, ohne im Schlüssel nachzuschauen. Wenn Sie bei der Kontrolle feststellen, daß Sie

Vorwort

viele Fehler gemacht haben, lassen Sie sich dadurch bitte nicht deprimieren. Aus Fehlern kann man eine ganze Menge lernen. Am besten lesen Sie dann die Erklärungen noch einmal und machen die Übungen entweder gleich oder am nächsten Tag noch einmal bzw. so lange, bis Sie ganz sicher sind. Es empfiehlt sich, über die Lückentexte eine Folie zu legen und darauf zu schreiben. Dann können Sie diese Übungen bei Bedarf wiederholen.

Wir erwarten nicht, daß Sie das Buch auf einmal von A bis Z durcharbeiten. Aber es reicht natürlich auch nicht, wenn Sie es sich nur unters Kopfkissen legen. Sprachenlernen ist nicht immer ein reines Vergnügen. Trotzdem haben wir versucht, unser Buch so zu schreiben, daß es Ihnen auch Spaß macht.

Hannelore Nuffer

Frank Steele

Noch ein Hinweis:

An einigen Stellen des Buches (besonders z. B. in dem Kapitel „An American Education“) finden Sie auch amerikanisches Englisch (Am. E.). Es wird in vielen Fällen, wo Am. E. im Buch auftaucht, nicht mehr auf die orthographischen Unterschiede hingewiesen, da wir davon ausgehen, daß sie auf diesem Niveau weitgehend bekannt sind. Sollten Sie trotzdem einmal Zweifel haben, schlagen Sie bitte in einem guten Wörterbuch nach.

Inhalt

Inhalt

Starting off on the Right Foot

Expressing Your Own Opinion

Some Common Phrases to Begin Your Paragraphs or Sentences

Most written examinations you will face in English have as their starting point a text. You will probably be asked to answer some questions and comment on some points and opinions stated in the text. To make a connection between the question asked and your answer it is not often very good to simply repeat the question. Instead, you will want to shorten the reference with phrases like:

A) Laut Autor . . .
B) Nach Meinung des Autors . . .
C) Die Verfasserin ist der Auffassung, . . .
D) In dem Text wird behauptet, . . .

If you can readily translate these phrases into English you may want to move on to another section. This chapter is about how and when just such phrases are used.
First, let's translate and give examples of the German phrases above:
But before we begin, go back and try to work them out yourself. Now compare:

A) Laut Autor . . .
According to the author, English tests often begin with a text.

B) Nach Meinung des Autors . . .
In the author's opinion it is better when taking a comprehension examination not to restate the entire question.

C) Die Verfasserin*) ist der Auffassung, daß . . .
The writer is of the opinion that many students need help with lead-in phrases.

D) In dem Text wird behauptet, daß . . .
In the text it is claimed that you will have to comment on the author's opinions.

Notice that the last two phrases (C and D) are usually followed by the word *that.* And, you will notice, unlike the German equivalent daß it does not have a comma before it.

Expressing Your Own Opinion

Of all the phrases above only one is useful when you need a lead-in for expressing your <u>own</u> opinion. It is a varia-

---

*) The word *authoress* exists but is rare. One should have a good reason for emphasizing the sex of a particular writer, as in the case of the female writer, George Sand, for example. Her name was a pseudonym.

tion of a phrase above. Do you know which one? Well, it is a very formal and elegant phrase, but that is the style of your written compositions — unless, of course, you are asked to write a friendly letter to a fellow student.

I am of the opinion that is the one meant. Here are some more phrases with similar meanings:

My idea is that all examinations should be short and not too difficult.
I believe (that) even educated English-speaking people would not get perfect marks on some of the English tests I have seen in Germany.
I think I would get better grades in my exams if I could listen to music while taking the exam.
I would say that English comprehension tests should have interesting themes.
Notice, if you expected to read ✗ I mean ✗ or ✗ My meaning is ✗ that is pure German interference from the words meinen/Meinung and has a different usage in English. We use *mean* or *meaning* when we want to clarify or interpret something we have already said. Do not use those words when you want to state your opinion or belief!
(→ chapter 2, p. 14)

Did you also notice that a couple of times the phrase appeared *to take an examination?* In English, someone gives you an examination and you take it. Hence:

take a test —
When are you going to take your driving test?
After I took the eye examination the doctor said I needed glasses!
He had to take the pilot's exam twice. He failed the first time.
The mistake we frequently see is ✗ to make an examination ✗ . In English this would mean to create or develop an exam, e. g.: A committee of teachers made a terribly hard geography test which all the students failed.

To return to the subject, we also need special lead-ins when we want to finish what we are saying on a topic. Words like:

Zusammenfassend . . .
  To summarize/In sum/To sum up, . . .
Abschließend . . .
  To conclude,/In conclusion, . . .
Zuletzt . . .
  Finally, . . .
Notice, the words or phrases here are followed by a comma!

A Miscellany of Confounded Words
German-English Mix-ups

The following list of words and phrases is based on mistakes made by students who wrote answers to comprehension test questions. The mistakes resulted from translations of German words which have more than one meaning in English. Study the examples carefully.

Bank = bank & bench

I borrowed money from the *bank*. I *bank* (habe mein Konto) at the Bank of America.

We sat on a *bench* in the park. (Eckbank = corner bench *or* nook bench is not a very common piece of furniture in English or American households.)

bemerken = notice & remark

She *noticed* that close friends in England did not usually shake hands. She *remarked* to her husband about this seemingly strange custom. (The former is to see and the latter is to say something.).

bequem = comfortable & convenient

They felt quite *comfortable* sitting in the leather chairs. He led an easy and *comfortable* life, leaving the work to others. (*Convenient* has the idea of being suitable, handy or nearby.) It's more *convenient* to eat at the canteen than to go home for lunch. The new house was *conveniently* located — all the stores were within walking distance. Is 10:00 a. m. a *convenient* (passend) time for our appointment?
Public conveniences are toilets available for use by everyone. A newly built apartment with all the modern conveniences.
Antonyms: uncomfortable & inconvenient.

(sich) blamieren = to make a fool of someone (oneself); sich blamiert fühlen = to feel embarrassed

It does not mean 'to blame'. *Blame* means tadeln, die Schuld geben, verantwortlich machen.
He *blamed* himself for causing the accident. The government tried to *blame* the rise in unemployment on the unions; the unions' reply was that the government's

inflation policy was at fault. Don't *blame* me for the parking ticket; I told you not to park there!
He *made a fool of himself* after drinking so much at his first wife's second wedding. The teacher *felt embarrassed* because she wasn't sure how to spell the word 'accommodate'.

Boden = soil/earth & ground & floor & the bottom (of a container)

The *soil* rich in minerals, the *earth* just ready to be ploughed *(= Br. E.;* plowed *= Am. E.)* It was autumn *(= Br. E.;* fall *= Am. E.)* and the dark red apples were about to drop onto the *ground.* Do we have to wax the *floors* every Saturday? The wine in the barrel was almost finished and there were fine crystals all over the *bottom.* (→ p. 134 "The Plain Truth, etc.)

böse = angry & naughty & bad & evil

She was *angry* with me because I had forgotten our anniversary. The children had thrown food all over the floor and their mother told them they were *naughty.* (Usually only used for children = ungezogen, unartig.)
Bad is a general term for anything reprehensible (verabscheuenswert), *evil* is stronger, meaning sinister or morally reprehensible: The evil that men do lives after them — just being bad will not make you famous.

bringen → tragen

Brunnen = fountain & well

The beautiful *fountains* to be found in the squares of Rome. He drank the fresh

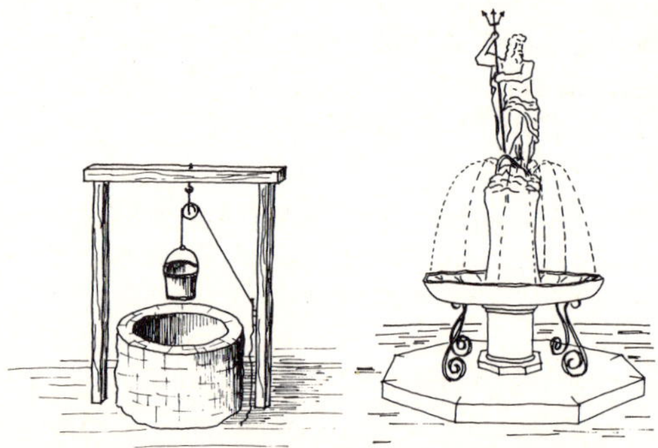

water from the *well.* (A *well* is underground. Also, an oil well, which is a hole made to get oil from underground.)

dick = thick & fat

A book can be *thick,* meaning it has many pages. A sauce can be *thick,* or *thick* slices of tomato. (A thick person = doof, i. e., unable to understand.)
To call someone *fat* is a not very polite way of saying he is overweight.

engagiert = involved, committed & occupied, busy, engaged

It is very difficult to separate the above words in meaning. But current German usage, i. e., Ein engagierter Lehrer; er engagiert sich sehr für die Friedensbewegung, cannot simply be translated

A Miscellany of Confounded Words

by: An *engaged* teacher; but perhaps: he is very *engaged* in the peace movement. Current English usage would probably translate: A teacher very *involved* in his students and educational ideas. He is *committed* to the environmental improvement of his country. Often, *engaged* is similar to *busy* or *occupied (with)* in the sense of beschäftigt. *Involved* and *committed* have the added sense of *dedicated* or *devoted*, which have very positive connotations, which cannot be found in the sense of being *busy*. Engaged = verlobt: She was engaged to be married and wore an engagement ring.

> ! involved *in*
> engaged *in*
> but: committed *to*

erinnern = remember & remind

I *remember* seeing your face. (I have not forgotten; I recall it now.) Your face *reminds* me of the Mona Lisa. (Seeing you brings back something I had forgotten and now, suddenly, it comes back to mind.) Most often the error is in construction: one thing *reminds* me *of* something else; I am *reminded of* the time I spent in the Alps. (For constructions with *remember*, → p. 81 "Gerunds")

Erziehung = education & upbringing

erziehen = to educate & to bring up, to raise, to rear

Education takes place in educational institutions and is done by educators, i. e., teachers. *Upbringing* is the responsibility of parents and has less to do with imparting (vermitteln) knowledge than with inculcating (einprägen, einimpfen) manners, spirit, attitudes and principles in children. *Education* is a lifelong process; *upbringing* is not. Certainly, also in English, the two overlap slightly in reality, but hardly in usage. I was *raised* by my parents to be a good Christian. I was *brought up* to be a well-mannered and polite lady. To *rear* emphasizes discipline and is also applied to animals. (→ An American Education, p. 148)

Fehler = mistake & fault

A *mistake* is something you make, while *fault* means either a defect, i. e., a built-in error, or blame as in : "It was my *fault* we were late." "After the car accident, the police tried to determine who was at *fault.*" So when you write a paper or a test, you cannot speak of the teacher correcting the *faults,* but *mistakes* can be corrected. A *fault* is simply there, as in: "The dress was marked down because it had a *fault* in the collar."

Frau = woman & wife

Woman is the general term. Use *wife* in connection with a possessive pronoun: *his wife, my wife, their wives.* Wife = Ehefrau. We looked at the *women* standing in line for bread. There was no way he could stop his *wife* from learning a new language. (→ below, "Mann") By the way, the word for the other married person — regardless of gender — is *spouse* (= Gatte, Gattin).

Geschichte = story & history

My children love Micky Mouse *stories*. She told me the *story* of her life in South Africa.
History is the study of significant events in the past. A *history* of Germany in the 20th century written by K. S. Pinson. *History* attempts to find the truth, while *stories* make no such claim. (As persons: historians; storytellers).

groß = big, large & tall & great

Big and *large* are the general terms: a *big* lake, a *large* fortune. *Tall* refers to vertical largeness: a *tall* woman, a *tall* building. *Great* means classically import-ant, famous and significant: the *great* composer, Brahms; the *great* temples of Greece; the *great* books of all times by Proust, Hawthorne and Darwin.
Bismarck was a *large, tall* and *great* man. When he died he weighed over 270 pounds, was more than six feet in height and now is considered a key figure in German history. When we say, "That was a *great* party," we are using the word colloquially.

Karte = map & card

A map = Landkarte. We have a *map* of Italy to find our way. *Card* is a thick piece of paper, e. g., *post card*, greeting *cards* for Christmas, birthdays, etc., playing *cards* for poker and other *card* games. (Mappe = briefcase; Speisekarte = menu!)

kochen = boil & cook

We *boil* water, the water is *boiling*, hence we can *boil* eggs for breakfast or for making Easter eggs, i. e., hot bubbling liquid. We *cook* a meal; she is *cooking* dinner; don't *cook* the food too long or it will lose its vitamins.

kontrollieren = control & check

For control use beherrschen and for check use überprüfen. She couldn't *control* the children's behavior. He had everything under *control*, nothing happened without his permission. Attendant, please *check* the oil and water. Just let me *check* that the heater is turned off before we go.
Remember *Checkpoint* Charlie where they *check* your passports.

Land = country & land

America is a beautiful *country*. It is the *country* I come from. I live *in the country* (= auf dem Lande), not very far from the city. Sometimes, *land* is used to mean country, but that is poetic or literary

A Miscellany of Confounded Words

usage: Canada, the *land* of my dreams. The farmer had a lot of *land* (= much property). It was good *land* for grazing cattle (= suitable space and soil). In studies or reports on Germany, *Land* and *Laender* is understood among experts (i. e., Bavaria, Lower Saxony, Rhineland-Palatinate (Rheinland-Pfalz), etc.).

lassen = let, allow & leave & have something done

Let is the general term, while *allow* adds the idea of authority; and both have the sense of giving permission. *Let* him alone, don't bother him. (Also, *Leave* him alone = a variation of the above.) Her mother *let* her stay out late. The police wouldn't *allow* them to get in. *Let* me see that. Am I *allowed* to take that book along?
Leave the dishes for me to do. *Let* me do the dishes. She *left* the dishes for the maid to wash. She *let* her friend help her wash up.
I *had* my shoes repaired. I *had* my hair washed. I have to *have* the car fixed. (= etwas machen lassen)

leihen = lend, (loan) & borrow

lend, lent, have lent. (more often *Am. E.)* loan, loaned, have loaned.
From Shakespeare's <u>Hamlet</u>: Polonius' advice to Laertes –

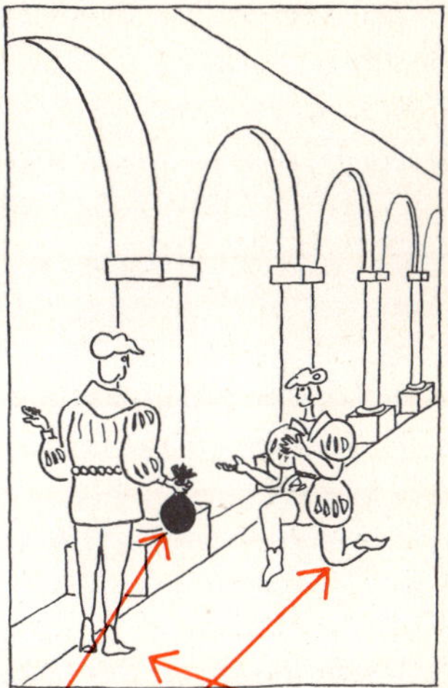

"Neither a borrower nor a lender be;
For loan oft loses both itself and friend,"
I *borrowed* these books from the library. The library *lent* them to me. Can I *borrow* these from you? Yes, I can *lend* them to you. Would you like to *borrow* these from me? Would you *lend* them to me?
You have probably guessed: borrow from & lend to. But it is not always explicitly stated. Sometimes it is implicit, as in: Can I *borrow* these? Can you *lend* my sister those? I *borrowed* them.
Try this short exercise:

A. I want to ________________ these tools for a week. I'll return them on time.

B. I'll never ________________ him anything again. He never brings it back.

A. borrow; B. lend

A Miscellany of Confounded Words
German-English Mix-ups

locker = loose
lösen = loosen
verlieren = lose

The screw was *loose* so he tightened it with a screwdriver. After the party he *loosened* his tie and fell asleep in a chair. Please don't put all that money in your shirt pocket. You'll *lose* it! (The above is nominated as a candidate for the TOP 10 most common mistakes in exams. The source of error, probably, is not the German, but mispronunciation. Please read them out loud:

loose	loosen	lose
[lu:s]	['lu:sən]	[lu:z]

Listen to the 's' & 'z' sounds!)
Don't lose points for making careless mistakes. If you misspell *lose* too often, your teacher will think you have a screw loose.

Mann = man & husband

It is more common to say: "Married men want their wives to do the housework," than to begin with "Husbands". The word usually refers to a relationship with someone else, hence its usual connection with possessive pronouns. (→ Frau, above). It is not Standard English to speak of "my man" or "his woman" in the sense of husband or wife, although it is often heard in songs, like the line from Gershwin's Porgy and Bess: "Bess, you is my woman now." Unless you are singing, stay with *husband* and *wife*. Should you get married in English you will hear the phrase: "I now pronounce you man and wife." = Bible. *Man* is also used as mankind, as in: *Man* is evolving. But: "What *men* will do about the atom bomb," might not be well-received by feminists.

meinen & Meinung = think & mean & opinion

(→ p. 7 "Starting Off on the Right Foot") If you just want to say "Ich meine . . .," then "I think . . .," or "I believe . . .," (= Ich glaube . . .) is the easiest way of rendering that phrase. *"I mean . . .,"* is used as an interpretation or further explanation of what has already been said. I *think* solving the unemployment problem will require sacrifices. I *mean* that everyone will have to be satisfied with less money. What that *means* is that for everyone to have work, all working people will probably have to work fewer hours per week or even retire at an earlier age.

You can forget about phrases with ✗ my meaning, their meaning, etc. ✗ in the sense of *what I think, what their opinion is.* It's not English! *Meaning* has the sense of giving a definition or explanation, especially of something hidden or hard to understand. "What is the English *meaning* of Gemütlichkeit?" Philosophers are preoccupied with finding the *meaning* of life.

A Miscellany of Confounded Words

When you want to say, "Seine Meinung . . . ," use, "His opinion . . ."
I think those *opinions* need more evidence. In my *opinion* you don't have any idea about the real *meaning* of what you are saying. I'm tired of listening to your ridiculous *opinions,* can't you just say what you *mean.* What I *meant* was, couldn't you get to the point?

mögen = like & want

I like whisky but I don't want any for breakfast.

I would like = I want. I would have liked = I wanted.

They would have liked to have seen Disneyland, but they also wanted to lie in the sun on the beach.
Would like is more polite in questions: *Would you like* a cup of tea? Among friends one would probably say: *Do you want* some coffee? *Want* is simply more direct, as in: He *wanted* a job desperately (= brauchte).

Nachricht = news & message

The *news* is on television at 8:00 o'clock. Have you heard the latest *news* about Princess Diane? There's no *news* like bad *news* (saying). "I'm sorry, Mr. Johnson isn't in at the moment. Can I take a *message?"* "Yes, I'd like to leave a *message* for Mrs. Johnson."
Is there any *news* about her grandmother's health? The last report I got was that she was in critical condition.

nächst = next & nearest

Next implies an order of things as on a list. "That's the second time you've missed an appointment. The *next* time will be the last time." What's the *next* item of business on the agenda? A receptionist in a doctor's waiting room calling for another patient: *"Next,* please." Also used for people living next door, as in: my next-door neighbour.
Nearest means closest in distance or time. "I'm looking for the *nearest* taxi stand." The *nearest* building is ten miles away. (Cf. latest and last: The latest fashions = the most recent; the last stop on the subway *(Am.E.;* underground = *Br.E.)* = final in an order.) (See also p. 52).

passen = fit & suit & match

In the figurative sense *fit* & *suit* are often synonymous, as in: Words which *fit/suit* the occasion; *fitting/suitable* remarks.
However, when speaking of clothing: The jacket *fits* well = it is the right size. That hat *suits* you = appropriate to someone's personality or style. *Matching* jacket and trousers *(Br.E.;* pants, *Am.E.)* = identical in colour or pattern (not clashing).

A Miscellany of Confounded Words
Exercise

Politik = politics & policy

The former means Staatsangelegenheiten or Parteipolitik, as in: Analyzing the *politics* of socialist governments; studying *politics* as a university subject; "Let's not talk about *politics* or religion"; she favours liberal *politics*. Whereas *policy* refers to Programm or Taktik, as in: the party's *policy* on abortion; our school's *policy* on smoking in the classroom; they were not sure which *policy* to adopt in regard to atomic energy. Thus, it can also mean Prinzip. In a formal figurative sense: It was my father's *policy* never to lend out his car. The President's closest advisers and policy makers realized that women's liberation had become a political issue.

(Politiker = politician)

Quelle = spring, well, source & origin, source & authority, source (→ Brunnen)

The *source* of the Rhine is in the Alps. The Rhine is the *source* of many sailors' livelihood. His *source* of information was in the White House itself. Jesus talked to the women at the *well*.
Fresh *spring* water is bottled and sold.

The *origin (source)* of wisdom is knowledge. When writing scientific papers, be sure to cite your *authorities (sources)*.

rauben = rob/steal

Shared meaning: to take something of value from a person or place unlawfully.
The main difference is in usage.
— to rob someone or something <u>of</u> something
— to steal something <u>from</u> someone or something

They just *robbed* Barclay's Bank. They *stole* a million pounds in cash.
The National Museum was *robbed* last night. They *stole* the golden mummy.
Barclay's Bank was *robbed of* a million pounds. One million was *stolen from* Barclay's Bank.
The museum was *robbed of* its golden mummy. The mummy was *stolen from* the museum.

Exercise 1:
Fill in using the passive of *rob* or *steal* (always past tense, here):
Example:

money *was stolen* ____________

a. bank ____________

b. traveler's checks ____________

rob = followed by <u>who</u> was robbed: a jewelry store, a person, a bank.
steal = followed by <u>what</u> was stolen: paintings, money, a wallet, furs.

A Miscellany of Confounded Words Exercise

c. museum ______________________

d. gold ______________________

e. coins ______________________

f. salesmen ______________________

g. books ______________________

h. time ______________________

i. candy ______________________

j. passengers ______________________

(→ p. 48, "Crime and Punishment")

Rezept = recipe ['resɪpɪ] & prescription

I have a good *recipe* for stuffed mushrooms. The chef's *recipe* for fish.
The doctor gave me a *prescription* for penicillin.

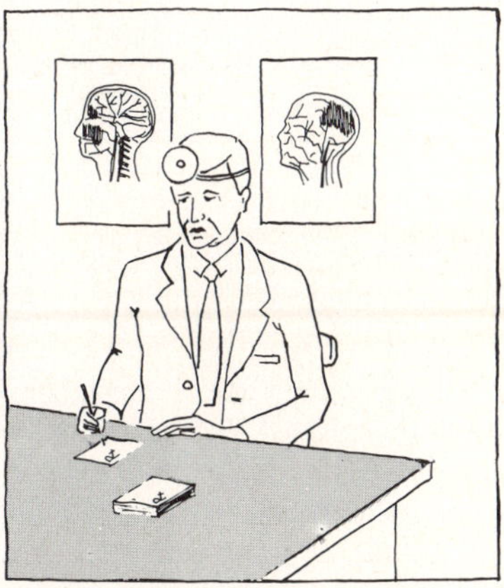

Both are used figuratively to mean directions or a remedy to cure a problem, as in: What's your *recipe/prescription* for a good marriage?

sagen = say & tell

To *say* something is to open your mouth and express something, whether or not anyone is listening, as in: I always *say*, let sleeping dogs lie.
She *said* she wouldn't be home in time. (The listener is unknown.)
I *told* them about my trip to Yugoslavia. She *told* me it was late. (The listener is always mentioned.)
(Speak adds the idea of more formal talking, as in a speech.)

Schatten = shade & shadow

In common usage *shade* implies shelter or protection from light or heat, as in: We were sitting in the *shade* of the old oak tree.
Whereas *shadow* denotes the figure produced by blocking light, as in: We walked along watching the *shadows* produced by our bodies.
Both words mean relative darkness. *Shadows* have definite shapes, while *shade* is diffuse. *Shadow* might be regarded as part of *shade*, i. e., as smaller, darker, clearer.

Spiel = play & game & match & gambling

A *play* by Shakespeare performed in London; the characters in the *play*.
A *game* of football played in a stadium; the athletes in the *game*.
A volleyball *match* between two rival

schools; the two teams in the *match.*
Poker is a card game I like to play but *gambling* a lot of money on it is not my idea of fun.
Play as a noun almost always refers to a stage play or drama. As a verb it can refer to sports, athletics, games; the actors *played* their parts well; he *played* roulette and won; she *plays* the piano; stop *playing,* this is serious, i. e., *play* has a basic meaning opposite of earnest.
Game has no verb form and thus needs *play,* as in: Children play games.
Game and *match* have the idea of organized play with rules, especially *match* has the idea of an official game.

Stimme = voice & vote

To have a *voice* in politics is to have influence, express an opinion and thus is difficult to measure, whereas a *vote* in an election is a ballot cast and thus can be counted.
A *voice vote* in parliament: the members call out their approval or dissapproval by saying aye (= old form of yes) or nay (= old form of no). The ayes/nayes have it (= win = have the majority).
You can vote in American elections when you are 18 years old, but younger people have made their *voices* heard in politics.

Straße = road & street

A road is *between* cities or towns; a street is *in* cities or towns.

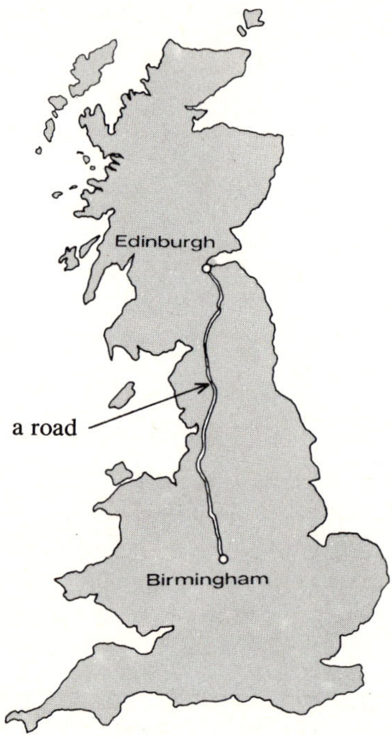

There is a good *road* between Los Angeles and San Diego, in fact it's freeway (= Autobahn) almost the whole way. *King's Road** is a fashionable street in London. The mountain *roads* were closed due to heavy snowfall. During rush hour, Boston's *streets* are jammed. [A highway *(Am. E.)* = Bundesstraße = a main direct road *(Br. E.);* freeway, tollway, expressway *(Am. E.)* = Autobahn = motorway, a divided highway *(Br. E.)]*

---

* Here *Road* is part of a proper name!

A Miscellany of Confounded Words

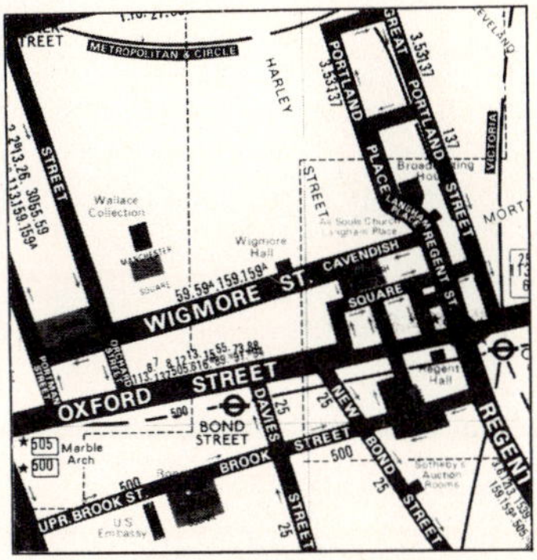

streets

Technik = technology & technique

(The -ch- in tech- is pronounced like -k-: [tek'nɒlədʒɪ], [tek'ni:k]).

Technology is the application of science to industry; or all the means a society uses to produce the objects it needs to live. Some people say that *technology* in the West, particularly its computers, genetic manipulation and space travel, needs more control by responsible politicians and less by technocrats.

Technique is used for methods or skills, ways of doing things = Verfahren, Fertigkeit, Arbeitsweise, as in: Jackson Pollack's *technique* of drip painting; Günther Grass's *technique* of recycling images and characters through several of his novels; a biochemical *technique* of isolating the nuclei of cells; he was sure he had discovered a new *technique* of kissing. (Technic & technics are rare and better left to technical specialists.)

Techniker = technician *or* engineer!

tragen = wear & carry & bear

Something *is worn* by a person, habitually, such as clothes or ornaments. To *carry* means to transport from one place to another and *bear* stresses that what is carried is heavy or difficult to transport or move, also in the figurative sense, as in: a tragic burden difficult to *bear;* to *bear* the weight of the world's sorrow on his shoulders.

For the party he *wore* his best suit, his newest tie and his most expensive aftershave. Whose sunglasses are you *wearing?*

Let me help you *carry* that box. On cloudy days he always *carried* an umbrella in the same hand as his briefcase; his raincoat was always *carried* over his arm until it actually began to rain; then he *wore* it indoors and outdoors until the weather cleared.

(*Carry* means to bring or take — remember that bring (= herbringen) means to carry from there to here & take (= hinbringen) means from here to there, both from the standpoint of the speaker.)

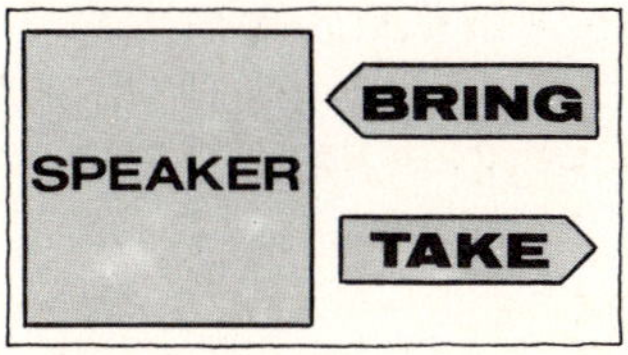

A Miscellany of Confounded Words
Exercise

Exercise 2:
Put a *W* next to the things usually worn and a *C* next to the things that are normally carried:

1. earrings ___	9. hat ___	17. wallet ___
2. umbrella ___	10. boots ___	18. skirt ___
3. suitcase ___	11. coin purse ___	19. vest ___
4. wig ___	12. medals ___	20. toupee ___
5. goggles ___	13. socks ___	21. crash helmet ___
6. wedding ring ___	14. teapot ___	22. pocket knife ___
7. axe ___	15. bath towel ___	23. swim trunks ___
8. beard ___	16. a smile ___	24. petticoat ___

wählen = choose & vote (for) & elect & dial

To *choose* (select or pick out = aussuchen) a career is not easy.
I *voted* for the best candidate, but she

was not *elected,* i. e., I cast my ballot for someone — my choice — but the voters as a whole did not choose the same person, so another person had more votes and was elected.

I *dialled* the dial on my telephone. The number you have dialled is out of order. Keep *dialling* until you get through.

Warenhaus = department store & (warehouse)

Bloomingdale's in New York is one of my favourite *department stores;* it's just more fun to shop there. They have lots of little shops inside, many more than Harrod's and much more individual. *Warehouses* (= Lagerhäuser) are places to store goods. You cannot buy anything there.

A Miscellany of Confounded Words Exercise

Exercise 3:
In the following put in the appropriate word in its appropriate form. Mind the tenses and endings!

1. (bank/bench)
   During a football game those players not on the field have to remain on the ______________. If I were you I wouldn't put all my cash in the ______________.
2. (notice/remark)
   Have you ______________ the trees are getting yellowish? Such ______________ should be kept to oneself. "If I thought the forests were actually dying," she ______________, "I would certainly get involved in trying to do something about it."
3. (comfortable/convenient)
   It is a ______________ feeling knowing that I will someday inherit the ranch. Living near an underground station is very ______________.
4. (embarrass/blame)
   I felt ______________ for my daughter after her teacher's remarks. I was ______________ for not giving her a proper upbringing.
5. (soil/ground/floor)
   They had been drinking champagne and now the ______________ was sticky. This is good ______________ for planting clover. The horse bucked and she crashed to the ______________.
6. (angry/naughty/bad/evil)
   The children had been ______________ and their mother got ______________. The war was ______________ enough but the concentration camps were absolutely ______________.

A Miscellany of Confounded Words
Exercise

7. (fountain/well)

Some of Italy's finest artists were involved in designing the lovely ____________. To poison the community ____________ is a classic example of unsocial behaviour.

8. (thick/fat)

Some people can eat and eat and never get ____________. Don't slice the bread too ____________.

9. (involved/committed/busy/engaged)

He had been ____________ before, but this time he really thought he would get married. He was ____________ to promoting peace and always ____________ reading books or lecturing. The more they heard, the more they realized they were becoming ____________ in criminal activities.

10. (remember/remind)

____________ me to take down the rubbish *(= Br. E.;* garbage = *Am. E.)* before we leave. Drinking retsina ____________ me of our vacation in Greece. I will always ____________ dancing in Greece.

11. (education/upbringing)

Their ____________ qualified them to go on to a higher paying job. Now that I have children of my own, I see there is much more involved in the ____________ of them than just providing them with good principles to live by.

12. (mistake/fault)

I don't know who is at ____________ for this, but I hope you never make this ____________ again.

13. (woman/wife)

I knew this was the ____________ of my dreams and I asked her to be my ____________. Our ____________ complained about the housework, so we

A Miscellany of Confounded Words Exercise

formed a team of men to watch the children and clean up every Saturday. Freud asked: "What do ______________ want?"

14. (story/history)
If you don't tell the children ______________, they'll never go to sleep. To understand the war you have to read the ______________ of Vietnam.

15. (large/tall/great)
I couldn't really tell you how ______________ redwood trees grow but they're very old when they get that high. ______________ crowds do not always mean the speaker is popular. It is too early to say whether Helmut Schmidt will later be considered a ______________ chancellor.

16. (map/card)
Some families in the U.S.A. like to hang up the Christmas ______________ they receive on a door. Let's get a ______________ of Turkey before we drive there.

17. (boil/cook)
When the water is ready put the eggs in to ______________ for three minutes. She likes to ______________ and everyone enjoys it when she does.

18. (control/check)
There's no way to ______________ cattle in a thunderstorm. I wish you would ______________ your test papers before handing them in and ______________ that your name is at the top.

19. (country/land)
In this ______________ the press is controlled by financial interests. How much ______________ do you need for growing corn and raising sheep?

A Miscellany of Confounded Words
Exercise

20. (let/leave/have something done)

It's dirty and I want to ____________ it washed. I ____________ them wash it because they were having so much fun. When they're done, let's ____________ them some money and go.

21. (lend/borrow)

Would you like me to ____________ you my radio? You can ____________ it from me for a week.

22. (loose/loosen/lose)

If the wheel is ____________ you could ____________ it while driving. Just ____________ your tie, sit down and relax. You shouldn't hang around with ____________ women; once you ____________ your innocence it's gone forever.

23. (man/husband)

We don't know a single ____________ who would be suitable for our daughter. When I talk to your ____________ about it, he sees everything differently.

24. (think/mean/opinion)

I'm not sure I understand what you ____________ when you say you can't remember. The judge's ____________ expressed a minority viewpoint. We, the majority, ____________ she has a right to demonstrate on the steps of the Supreme Court.

25. (like/want)

When do you ____________ to finish the argument you started this morning? When I say I ____________ plums, it doesn't mean for breakfast, lunch and dinner!

26. (news/message)

There has been no ____________ about the Nobel Prize for literature for this year. Don't worry, dear, if they call you can be sure I'll leave a ______________ for you.

27. (next/nearest)

When's the ______________ train? Where's the ______________ toilet? Who do you think will be the ______________ Prime Minister? The ______________ time you call, ask the receptionist to notify me and I will run to the ______________ telephone.

28. (fit/suit/match)

If the shoe *(=Am. E;* cap *= Br. E.)* ______________, wear it (saying). Some people consider it very fashionable to wear scarves that ______________ the inside lining of their jackets or coats. I know some people will say your green hair is a bit extreme, but I think it ______________ your face and personality, just perfectly.

29. (politics/policy)

______________ decisions of that magnitude can only be made at the top. ______________ makes strange bedfellows. (Old English saying). At college he studied international ______________ and foreign ______________.

30. (rob/steal)

He ______________ Peter to pay Paul (Old saying). When you ______________ from a hospital, you are ______________ everyone. We don't know who ______________ your handbag, but the thief will be caught.

A Miscellany of Confounded Words
Exercise

31. (recipe/prescription)
My doctor has a masterful ____________ for baked cod and potatoes. This chemist's *(= Br. E.;* pharmacy = *Am. E.)* cannot sell narcotics to anyone without a ____________.

32. (say/tell)
We ____________ him we would be late. She ____________ he is always late, too. Marjorie just wouldn't ____________ everyone about what happened. Can you ____________ me the time?

33. (shade/shadow)
One of my favourite stories is by Plato. It is about people in a cave watching ____________ dancing on the wall. Diogenes said he wanted only one consideration: not to stand in his sunshine. I suppose he meant if he wanted ____________ he could sit under a tree.

34. (play/game/match)
Hey, old buddy, how about a ____________ of chess? We haven't ____________ for weeks. Did you see the fantastic championship chess ____________ on TV last night? The Soviet team won, as usual.

35. (voice/vote)
Now that the ____________ have been tallied (= counted), we can print the results of the election. "A lone ____________, crying in the desert." Keep your ____________ down, the baby is sleeping. If I thought any of the candidates would make a difference in my life, I would tell you who I was going to ____________ for.

36. (road/street)
I'm looking for the ____________ to Mexico City. I see, I turn left at the next

A Miscellany of Confounded Words Exercise

lights, then the third ______________ to the right, and there's the entrance to the freeway. Thanks.

37. (technology/technique)

He's anything but a virtuoso on the piano, it's all ______________ with him. High ______________ electronics has now become a major security problem for the military. Border guards are trying out new ______________ for detecting drugs.

38. (wear/carry/bear)

I just can't ______________ the excitement. Another dinner party, and I have absolutely nothing to ______________! Please ______________ my hat box to the coach, Jeeves.

39. (choose/vote (for)/elect/dial)

Schools cannot ______________ a profession for you. But if you ______________ the Labour Department's number, you will hear a recording full of advice. When Roosevelt was ______________ in 1932, nobody thought he would run for office three more times. If he were alive today, I know many who would still ______________ for him.

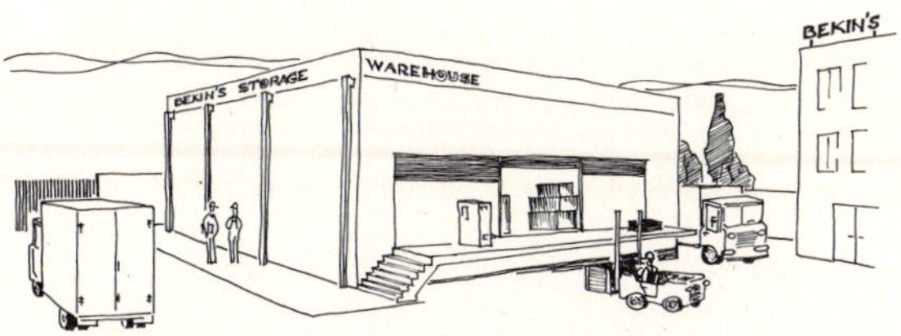

40. (department store/warehouse)

Before he moved to Dallas, he put all his furniture, clothes and sports equipment in a ______________ because he was sure it would otherwise be stolen. Then he went to one of the largest and cheapest ______________ and had himself outfitted in the tackiest western clothes ever seen by a cowboy.

Articles
Indefinite Article

Indefinite Article

You will certainly remember that the indefinite articles are *a* or *an* and that you use *a* when the word begins with a consonant or *an* when it has a vowel at its beginning. Now let's see how that works – TEST YOURSELF: Put *a* or *an* before the following words:

___ orange	___ biscuit
___ flame	___ house
___ honest man	___ H-bomb
___ underground	___ U.S. citizen
___ one-man show	

Have you got it right? Perhaps a little tricky:

an orange	a biscuit
a flame	a house
an honest man	an H-bomb
an underground	a U.S. citizen
a one-man show	

Although *honest* and *H-bomb* begin with a consonant and *U.S.* and *one-man* with a vowel in writing, we say *an honest man* and *an H-bomb* because we speak ['ɒnɪst] and ['eɪtʃ-]. On the other hand it's *a U.S. citizen* and *a one-man show,* because the pronunciation is ['ju:ˌes-] and ['wʌnmən]. So we can establish the following rule:

> *a* is used for words which begin with a consonant *sound;*
> *an* is used for words which begin with a vowel *sound;*
> What matters is the pronunciation, not the spelling!*)

Exercise 1:
Put in *a* or *an.*

1. "I'd like to live in ______ European country for a while", says Sue Mason, ______ university student at the Massachusetts Institute of Technology.
2. He is ______ unimaginative person and has ______ one-track mind.
3. We have always sent her ______ X-mas *(= Christmas)* card, why not this year?

---

*) By the way, the same rules apply for the pronunciation of the definite article *the* as [ðə] or [ðɪ] respectively.

Indefinite Article Exercises

4. Have you ever seen _____ UFO?
5. He had _____ heart attack and was taken to _____ hospital which specialised in heart diseases, but _____ hour later he was dead.
6. He is _____ honour to his profession.
7. In England you attach _____ L-plate to the front and the back of your car to show that you are learning to drive.

Now let's have a look at the usage of the indefinite article. You won't have many problems here, as many points are similar to German usage. So we'll pick out just a few things you may find difficult. Here are some rules:

> You always use the indefinite article to indicate somebody's profession, you don't use it if you want to indicate somebody's position, e. g.:
> He is a teacher. He is now personnel [–––´] manager of Unitrans.

Exercise 2:

Say what people do for their living.

He/She is _____

1

2

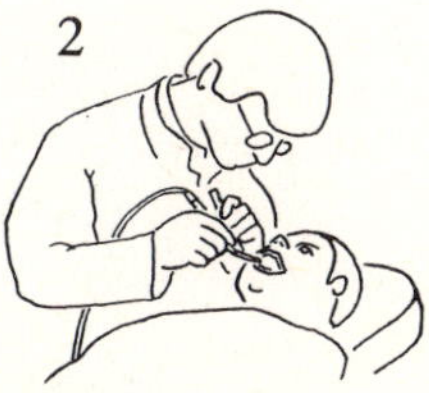

3

4

5

6

Articles
Indefinite Article

You always use the indefinite article before certain numerals:
a dozen, a hundred, a thousand,
a million.

You can also say *one* dozen, *one* hundred, etc., if you want to emphasize the figure.

! You also use the indefinite article with *half*, but you put it *after* the word: half a bottle of whisky, half an hour, etc.

You never use the indefinite article with uncountable nouns, such as *advice, news, information,* etc.*)

This is certainly a problem for German speakers, because in German you can say ein guter Rat which is *good advice* in English. So keep the following in mind:

!

ein guter Rat	= good advice
eine gute Nachricht	= good news
eine wichtige Information	= important information
was für ein Unsinn	= what nonsense
was für ein Glück	= what luck
was für ein Wetter	= what weather

But you say:
What *a* pity, what *a* shame = wie schade

Exercise 3:
Put in the indefinite article where necessary.

1. He is _____ plumber by trade.
2. I've told you _____ hundred times to close the door when you leave the room.
3. Have you heard that he has become _____ sales manager of Westbury Ltd.?
4. "I can't go out dressed like this!" — "What _____ nonsense! You look fine."
5. That was certainly _____ bad news.
6. "How much do the apples cost?" — "47 pence _____ pound, sir."

---

*) → Mass Nouns, p. 35

7. "I won't be able to come to your party tomorrow night." — "Oh, what _____ pity!"
8. Would you like to be _____ President of the United States?
9. I wouldn't like to be _____ teacher these days.

There is one other usage of the indefinite article we would like to point out. It is used to translate the German word pro: Ten times *a* minute/day/week/month/year; The cherries cost 95 cents *a* pound. He works at McDonald's two days *a* week. The car does at least 90 miles *an* hour.
Sometimes pro is translated by *per*, as in: m.p.h. = miles per hour.

Definite Article

The definite article has got only one written form, namely *the*, which is pronounced [ðə] when the word begins with a consonant sound and [ðɪ] when it begins with a vowel sound. (For pronunciation rules see above)

So let's get to the usage right away. Would you like to do a little test again? Put in *the* where necessary.

We arrived at _____ Heathrow Airport.

I live in _____ Half-Moon Street.

He goes to _____ church every Sunday.

We know _____ most people here.

I like _____ summer as much as _____ winter.

Did you put in *the* in one of the sentences? Well, that was wrong, I'm afraid. None of the sentences takes an article. Let's go into more detail. Look:

> Normally you don't use *the* before street names and proper names of buildings, airports, stations, etc.

You say for example: I arrived at Victoria Station/Kennedy Airport. When I was in London, I saw Buckingham Palace, Piccadilly Circus, Tower Bridge, Hyde Park, etc.
But you say *the* High Street, *the* Strand, *the* Mall, the latter two being famous streets in London.

Articles
Definite Articles

Exercise 4:
Imagine you are in London and have to describe the way from Victoria Station to the British Museum to an American. Here is the skeleton of what you would say. Put in all the names of buildings, streets, etc.

Go straight ahead. Pass ______. Then you go down ______ till you get to ______ Square. There you turn into ______

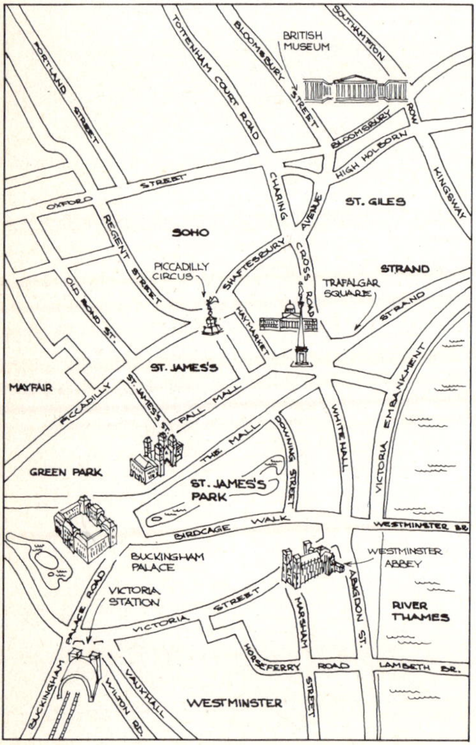

Road, cross ______ Avenue and shortly afterwards you'll hit ______ Street. Turn right and then left into ______ Street. And there you are, in front of the British Museum.

Now let's turn to something more difficult. Very often the use of the definite article depends on whether you use a word in a *general* or in a *specific* sense. This is particularly true for abstract words such as *love, nature, religion, motherhood, peace, life, industry, government,* and many, many more. When these words are used in a general sense, no article is required:
Love is wonderful. I enjoy nature. Freedom of religion is a basic right. In America all politicians say they are for motherhood and apple pie. We hope our children will always cherish peace. Life is beautiful. We prefer democratic government.

But when one speaks of these terms in a specific sense, they take the definite article:
The love of her life was named Alfred.
The religion of the Indians is Buddhism.
I don't like the life I am leading at the moment. The German Government has welcomed the proposal.

When considering whether the word needs a definite article or not, ask yourself: Is this a particular, special case of the word, different from other types of the same word? Look at these contrasts:

Definite Articles Exercises

general

He works in industry.
Safety and caution should be taught to young children.
All his life he loved music.

specific

The steel industry is having economic troubles.
The safety of pedestrians on zebra crossings cannot be guaranteed.
The music is too loud!

Sometimes, a good test of whether or not a word needs the definite article is to ask, could it also take *this* or *that,* words that clearly indicate a particular, specific instance. Try it here:

_____ system of taxation needs reform. _____ freedom is not absolute.
The first example needs an article because it is a certain sort of system, but the second example is a general idea and therefore needs no article.

The same rule applies to more concrete words as you can see from the following examples:

general

He went to bed early.
He always goes to church on Sunday.
We went to town yesterday.
He was sent to prison/hospital.
She goes to school/college/university.
I like spring/summer/autumn/winter best.
I always have cereal for breakfast.

specific

He lay down on the bed and fell asleep at once.
He went over to the church and admired the beautifully carved door.
We reached the town at noon.
They walked round the prison/hospital.
They are redecorating the school/college/university.
I remember the spring/summer/autumn/winter of 1980.
The breakfast at the hotel was rotten.

Home is always used without an article (we went home/stayed at home/came home early, etc.). But if it means Heimat, it takes an article, e. g.: India is the home of elephants.

Watch out for the following expressions because they differ from German in their use of the article!

Articles
Definite Articles

die meisten Leute	=	most people
die meiste Zeit	=	most of *the* time
alle Leute	=	all *the* people
Klavier/Geige etc. spielen	=	to play *the* piano violin etc.
er wusch sich die Hände	=	he washed *his* hands (→ p. 47)

Exercise 5:
Put in the definite article where necessary.

1. I do live near _____ airport, but not near _____ Heathrow airport. I live near _____ Gatwick airport.
2. If you want to play _____ piano well, you have to practise every day.
3. What the country needs is _____ strong government.
4. _____ Government have asked the country to decide by a vote.
5. I have known _____ most people in this department for a long time, but of course I don't know all _____ people in the firm.
6. I think in _____ spring _____ nature is at her best.
7. I think he lives in _____ Oxford Street.
8. Are you still at _____ school or do you go to _____ university already?
9. I don't like _____ hospital I work at, it's very old.
10. He caught a cold and had to stay at _____ home in _____ bed for a week.
11. Some people say that _____ happiness is not the most important thing in life.
12. In general I hate _____ winter, but _____ winter of 1977 was beautiful. That was when I first met John.
13. I work in _____ Main Street. As the name says, it's _____ main street of our town.
14. I read a new biography about _____ life of Napoleon.
15. _____ life is wonderful.

Nouns
Mass Nouns

*Mass Nouns = collective Nouns = uncountable Nouns = singular Nouns *)*

All of the terms above refer to a type of noun, e. g., *information* or *language,* which

1. almost never form a plural by adding *(e)s,* nor
2. do they take an indefinite article *(a* or *an)* and
3. they almost always can be made individual (or countable) by using *a piece of,* e. g., a piece of advice, two pieces of furniture.

Actually, a comprehensive list of mass nouns and their usages would be much too long and full of exceptions, so that as usual we will concentrate on the words most widely used and on the mistakes most frequently made.

You probably first met the problem of countable and uncountable when you learned the difference between much and many. Maybe the example used was:

much ice cream

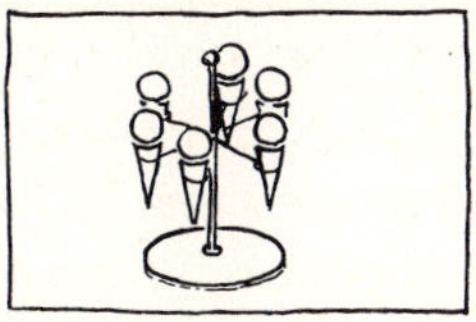

many ice cream cones

or:

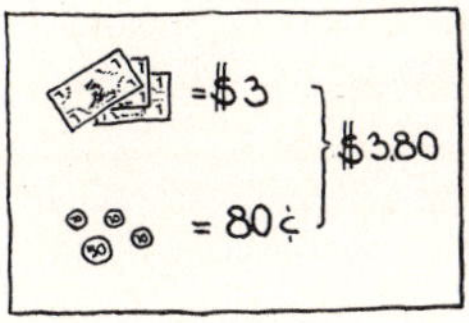

how much money (all together)

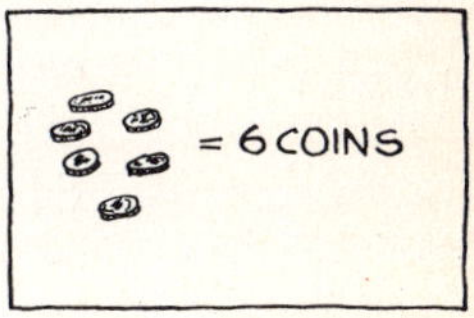

how many coins

Probably, the difficulty arises again because of what we have called German interference. Words like *information* or *news* cannot form a plural as in German Informationen or Nachrichten. In English we can form, though it is not all that frequent, several *pieces of information* were useful; many *pieces of news* do not get printed. I can give someone *some advice* or *some pieces of advice,* but I cannot say: ✗ an advice or one advice ✗ and, of course, I cannot give ✗ a few advices ✗ .

All mass nouns, then, cannot be used with *a* or *an, one, many* or *few* because these words show a number and those words, by definition, have no number.

Let's look at some more of them:
First, let's make a sub-division of mass nouns: abstract and concrete mass nouns.

*) auf Deutsch: nicht zählbare Substantive oder Gesamthauptwörter

Nouns
Mass Nouns

Abstract mass nouns:

information	advice
news	research
music	evidence
knowledge	progress
work *(=job)*	business *(= commerce)*

✗ a work ✗ just doesn't exist!

Concrete mass nouns:

luggage	baggage
furniture	equipment
machinery	paper
bread	chalk
meat	rice
hair	grass
sugar	salt
ice	snow
steel	iron

Wait a minute, you might be saying to yourself, you *can* say businesse*s* or bread*s*. But then you are talking about kinds or sorts of businesses or breads, e. g., Germany has wonderful (kinds of) breads. What businesses have closed down during this depression? As long as you are speaking of the word as a collective or a singular mass the rule applies. Now, go back through the lists of mass nouns above and ask yourself in German how the word would be formed in German as a singular and plural noun. Zum Beispiel, die Information — die Informationen; das Gepäck — die Gepäckstücke, usw. Eine Information = o.k., aber: ein Gepäck?
Go over each word like that, remembering in English, each time, it would perhaps be *some* equipment, *much* machinery, *a piece of* research, *an item of* business, *a bit of* work.

A Hairy Problem

He has a lot of hair. There's too much hair at the back. There's a hair in my soup. You have some loose hairs on your jacket. He cut three hairs off to examine them under the microscope. She used to have blonde hair, but now its black because her boy-friend likes black hair. And he only likes short hair.

Mass Nouns Exercise

Exercise 1:

Now you have a go at using some mass nouns in the singular. You will need to fill in the blanks with words such as: *piece, bit, type, slice, lump.*

Example: I don't want any blue paper. Don't you have __________ white paper?

Answer: *a piece of* or *a sheet of*

1. I don't like white bread. Can't I have _____ dark bread?
2. All that information was helpful, but there wasn't _____ information about the question I asked.
3. Bring the leather furniture up to my office, except for the two _____ blue velvet furniture which I want in the receptionist's lobby.
4. My father always had a lot of advice for me, but particularly _____ advice about raising children I never really understood.
5. There is not one _____ evidence to substantiate your claim!
6. You have not done one single _____ work since you moved in here last week!
7. Would you care for one or two _____ ice in your whisky?
8. I have not seen much progress since you started. In fact, unless you can show me one _____ progress, I think you'd better stop.
9. One _____ German machinery uses so much electricity they had to build a special power generator to keep it going. Other _____ Japanese equipment can be powered by small solar panels.
10. How many _____ sugar are you going to put in that coffee?
11. His last _____ research on "Labor Psychology and Cybernetics" was written up in the Los Angeles Times.

Nouns
Some Odd Plurals

Exercise 2:

Here are some odd pieces. Do you think the following sentences are correct or incorrect? Try and guess.

If you spill even one grain of salt, it is an awful waste.

I wish you had just one little shred of evidence to show that it was my client who committed the crime.

A hair in the sauce is like a piece of grass in your hair, though small everyone seems to notice it.

A little knowledge is a dangerous thing.

Some news have to be understood quickly.

Some Odd Plurals

Everyone knows that the English language has one of the largest vocabularies in the world. We are not sure if it is encouraging or discouraging for students learning this language to know that there are over 500,000 (five hundred thousand) words in general use, and there are estimates that when one includes all the words from technical subjects — i. e., chemistry, physics, linguistics, etc. — the English language comprises about 10,000,000 (ten million) words. At least we can be happy knowing that we — or anyone else for that matter — will never be burdened with having to store all those items in our memory. It is a sheer impossibility. In fact, even well-educated people go through life knowing less than 10% of the figure given for the common vocabulary.
This vast accumulation of words and phrases owes less to the creative powers of the English-speaking peoples than to its ability to borrow ably from the other languages of the world. "Real" English words, sometimes called Anglo-Saxon words, usually form plurals simply by adding an *"s"* sound. How often have you forgotten:

a word ending with 'y' forms a plural 'ies'?

For example: country/pl. countries; city/pl. cities; money/pl. monies (or moneys); family/pl. families; (just as the third person singular of cry is cries; fly is flies; and try is tries).
For every rule there is an exception: if there is a vowel before the 'y', then add 's'.
Examples: attorney/pl. attorneys; day/pl. days; monkey/pl. monkeys; and watch out for proper nouns, e. g., the two Germanys; many Kennedys; several

Nouns
Odd Plurals

Troys named after the historical city. Some others are: alley, boy, journey, key, valley and donkey.

In this book we will not cover mice and men, nor geese and oxen. The other Mentor Lernhilfen for English cover many of these problems already. Probably, only a careless mistake, but how often have we seen — instead of children — ✗ childs or childrens ✗ . And the plural of sheep is sheep and the plural of deer is deer. But we can't cover everything, so let's get back to problems our students have in common.
Having borrowed and retained words from various languages, the English-speaking peoples have apparently never come to grips with the pluralization of these words. Shouldn't we just treat them like good old English and give them an 's' or, on occasion, an 'es'? Wouldn't this finally demonstrate polite consideration for all the foreigners forced to struggle with all the other problems of learning this language? The answer is 'No' and 'Yes' — but the fact is, making English plurals has a few pitfalls.

The most common mistakes are made in taking a German plural for words that the German-speaking peoples have borrowed. The plural of *museum* is not ✗ museen ✗ and *stadium* does not produce ✗ stadia ✗ or ✗ stadions ✗ .

It's much too simple: *museums* and *stadiums* are the proper plurals. But watch out — from now on everything becomes confusing. Even the dictionaries and grammars differentiate between "common usage" and "technical usage" or "foreign usage", which only means that educated people (i. e., Standard English usage) tend to use the foreign or original plural and the masses use 's'. We are recommending Standard English, partly because the person correcting your examinations probably requires it.

—um → —a

medium/pl. media
Many politicians are worried about the growing power of the *media,* and television is the *medium* they are most concerned about.

Nouns
Some Odd Plurals

bacterium/pl. bacteria
It is very difficult to isolate one single *bacterium.* Medical hygienists tell us that smallpox *bacteria* are almost completely non-existent outside laboratories.

datum/pl. data
Datum used in the singular is quite rare; one would have to want to emphasize that it is one single bit of information. Computer *data* are used all over the world. (In scientific usage, when the information is seen as a block, one sometimes sees: This computer data *is* quite useful.)

—on → —a

criterion/pl. criteria
One *criterion* for assessing the value of a statement is its clarity. There are many *criteria* we use to judge the political stability of a State.

phenomenon/pl. phenomena
Lightning is a fantastic natural *phenomenon.* Empirical research relies on careful observation of *phenomena* occurring in the real world.

—is → —es

Another source of errors is the shift of words ending in 'is' to 'es'. These words stem from Greek and Latin roots.

crisis/pl. crises
The crisis over the Falkland Islands was solved by military force. The attention of the world has often turned to the crises in the Middle East.

thesis/pl. theses
Her doctoral thesis was written in 1964. Martin Luther posted his 95 Theses against the abuse of indulgences on a church door in 1517.

hypothesis/pl. hypotheses — antithesis/pl. antitheses
It was Charles Darwin's hypothesis that man had evolved from lower forms of life.
In dialectics, the antitheses are the opposites of hypotheses.

synthesis/pl. syntheses
Sigmund Freud's ideas were a synthesis of 19th century research in psychology and anthropology.

parenthesis/pl. parentheses
The punctuation symbols '(   )' are called parentheses though the British often say brackets, as well.

basis/pl. bases
(bases is also the plural of base)
The bases of his philosophy could be found in mystical religion, experimental physics and capitalist beliefs in individu-

Odd Plurals Exercise

alism. Bach's compositions form a basis for later classical music.

analysis/pl. analyses; psychoanalysis/ pl. psychoanalyses (rarely used)
Psychoanalysis is a therapeutic measure to cure mental illness. There have been many analyses of the causes of disease and some people believe that at the base of all illness lies a psychological factor.

Here is a list of a few more such words: axis/axes; diagnosis/diagnoses; neurosis/neuroses; oasis/oases; psychosis/psychoses; synopsis/synopses.

Exercise 3:
Write in the plurals of the following words

1. bacterium ________________
2. psychosis ________________
3. phenomenon ________________
4. datum ________________
5. child ________________
6. sheep ________________
7. crisis ________________
8. drama ________________
9. museum ________________
10. area ________________
11. territory ________________
12. monkey ________________
13. money ________________
14. dogma ________________
15. basis ________________
16. cow ________________
17. loss ________________
18. oasis ________________

Bits & Pieces

Did you know that 'rucksack', 'angst', and 'weltanschauung' are becoming acceptable English words? Although English speakers could almost as well say: 'backpack', 'anxiety', and 'world view'.

The Language of the Body
"Body" Idioms

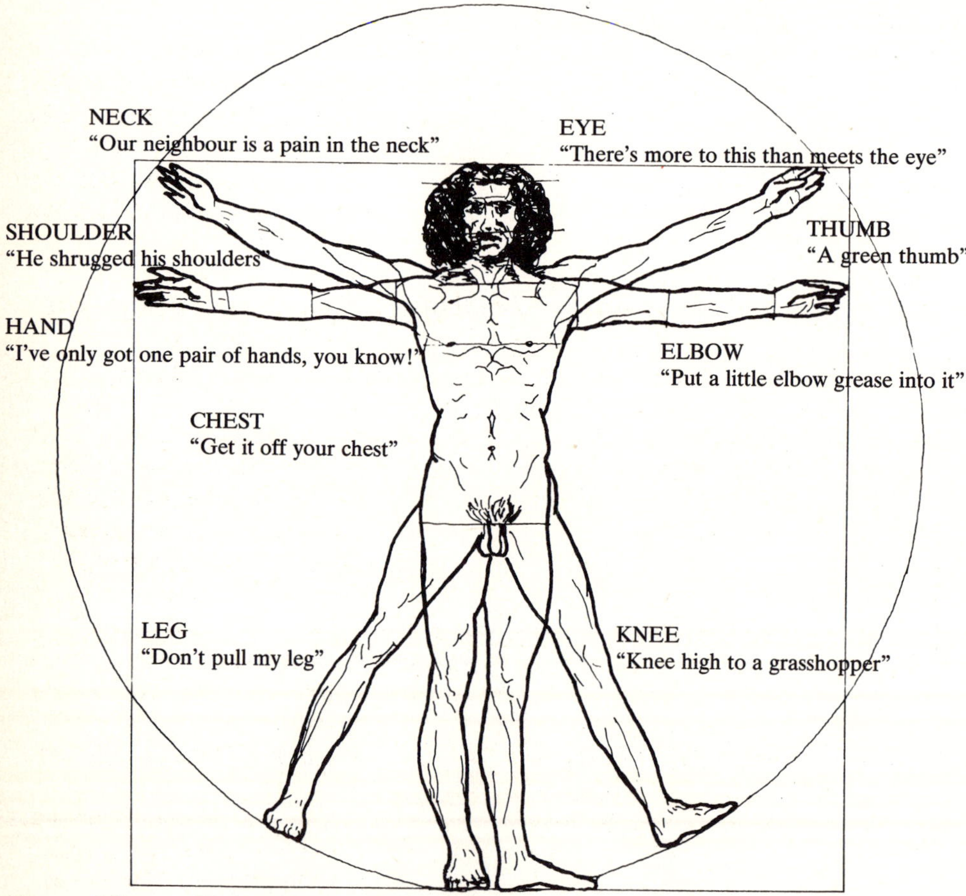

Some Idioms Using Parts of the Body

LEG:

- to pull someone's leg = jemanden auf den Arm nehmen
- shake a leg = hurry! get on with it!
- on one's/its last legs = worn out; tired
  a business on its last legs = almost bankrupt
- cost an arm and a leg = terribly expensive: Buying a house today costs an arm and a leg.

The Language of the Body
"Body" Idioms

NOSE:

- nosy = prying (neugierig im negativen Sinn)
- stick one's nose in other people's business = interfere
- right on the nose = exactly right; right on the button (Am. slang) His guess turned out to be right on the nose.
- turn one's nose up at something = to regard with scorn or disdain. Don't turn your nose up at good, wholesome food.

NECK:

- to neck = kiss, pet. They were seen necking in the car. (necken/Neckerei = to kid/kidding. It's only a joke, don't worry we were only kidding.)
- pain in the neck = lästig. All her advice was only a pain in the neck.
- to win by a neck = to be the winner by a close margin.
- breathe down someone's neck = to be following close behind, as in sports, or at work. The boss was breathing down his neck (= watching him closely).

EYE:

- to keep an eye on = to observe carefully The police were keeping an eye on the drug dealers, trying to follow their every move.

FOOT:

- my foot! = disagree strongly, as in: Finished! Finished my foot. You've just started.
- put one's foot down = be assertive, firm. Father said if you don't come home on time tonight, he's really going to put his foot down. You might have to stay home every night this month.
- put one's foot in it = blunder; to say or do something that offends or greatly irritates others.

The Language of the Body
"Body" Idioms

ELBOW:

- elbow grease = hard physical work; You'll never finish the floors at that rate. Put a little elbow grease into it!
- to elbow one's way = to elbow is a verb meaning to force one's way: He got to the top more with his elbows than his head, i. e., he elbowed his way to the top.

CHEST:

- get something off one's chest = to express one's worries, fears, troubles, complaints, etc.: Don't you think you would feel better if you talked about your problems, just to get them off your chest?

SHOULDERS:

- a shoulder to cry on (a shoulder to lean on) = offering sympathy and kindness to those who have problems: If I can't talk to anyone else, I know I can always cry on my father's shoulder. He always provided a shoulder to lean on.
- shrug one's shoulder = die Achseln zucken: He didn't know an answer and just shrugged his shoulders in bewilderment.
- chip on one's shoulders = to go around looking ready for a fight or an argument at the slightest provocation: Be careful today, he looks as if he has a chip on his shoulder; he's mad about the mess we made yesterday.
- give the cold shoulder to someone = express anger or disapproval by being silent or unfriendly: The employees were disgruntled about how their new boss had got his position and gave him the cold shoulder.
- to shoulder or to have on one's shoulders is often used figuratively in the sense of to bear: to shoulder responsibility; to have

the weight of family sorrows on his shoulders; you can tell her the bad news, she has strong shoulders (or broad shoulders) = she is not weak and can take the burden of the bad news.

HANDS:

- someone only has one pair of hands = one person can only do a certain amount of work at one time. A common reply when asked to do too much in a hurry.
- to take the law into your own hands = to punish wrongdoers without regard for legal codes or methods. (Extreme form = lynch justice.)
- give someone a hand = help someone: Can you give me a hand with these dishes.
- get out of hand = get out of control: The children are getting out of hand. Nuclear proliferation is getting out of hand.
- wash one's hands of = to attempt to deny or refuse responsibility: Pontius Pilate washed his hands of the crucifixion (= in the Bible he washed his hands clean of the affair publicly.) Nixon tried to wash his hands of the whole matter.
- the devil finds work for idle hands = If you don't find useful things to do you will get into mischief. (Old saying.)
- handy (handyman) = useful (useful person with his hands, especially in the household): It's always handy to have good tools around. I wish I had a dictionary handy (at hand = nearby).

The Language of the Body
"Body" Idioms

KNEE:

- knee high to a grasshopper = knee high to any small animal, i. e., a short person, especially a child: When I was knee high to a grasshopper, I couldn't say what I felt. (= when I was young and small.)

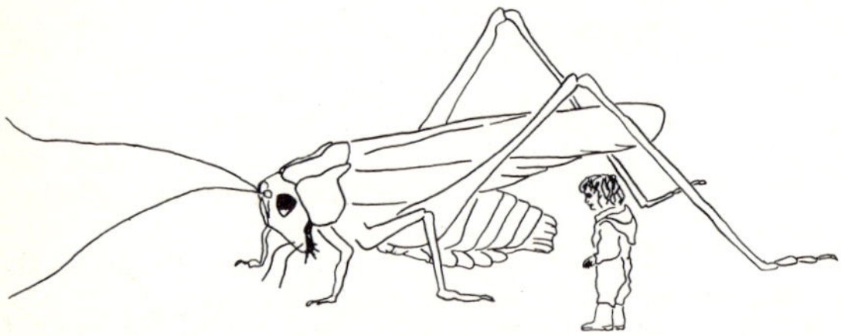

- bring someone to their knees = to defeat; also used for countries or armies.
- get down on one's knees = to beg
- someone's knees knock = show fear: She saw the giant and her knees began to knock and her teeth chattered.

Exercise 1:

Read through these sentences and try to understand the meaning of the idioms from the context.

Come on! *Shake a leg!* We can't be late for the party.

Don't be so *nosy!* It's none of your business why she's going to a psychotherapist. She shouldn't *stick her nose in other people's business.* I don't know why she told her friend that Jane had been given the sack.

I'm afraid this coat is *on it's last legs.* I guess it's time to buy a new one.

When they said you look awful in your new coat, they were just *pulling your leg.* In fact, it looks wonderful on you. You can see it must have *cost you an arm and a leg.* Just don't *turn your nose up at* good quality cloth; it will certainly last you a lifetime.

Listening to their jokes is sometimes a *pain in the neck.* You get the feeling they're always *breathing down your neck* with their sly remarks. Maybe we'll just have to *put our foot down* and tell them to watch their step. And *keep a close eye* on the Johnson twins; they're always starting the whispering and giggling. I really don't know what we can do *about* them. They're terrible. Last night they told the whole crowd they saw Dennis *necking* in a taxi with two women. I guess they thought it should have been them. The whole thing is *getting out of hand.*

"Body" Idioms Exercises

The parts of the body are used with the possessive pronouns: She has a key in her hand; the hat on his head; please keep your hands to yourself; they have nothing in their heads but nonsense.

Exception: He was stabbed in the back; He was shot in the knee. They stabbed him in the chest.

Naturally: I have a pain in my chest; hurt my toe; sprained my ankle.

And, by the way, when you have a headache, stomachache, earache or other pains, you may want to take some medicine for it. Someone might tell you to do something about your pains — like go and see a doctor; maybe he can do something about it. Fresh air is perhaps the best cure for most little aches and pains. (N. B. Rare with the preposition *against.)* Ah yes, one last thing: for heart*aches* maybe a good love story or some music might help you get over the romantic sorrow; for *pains* in the heart, see a doctor immediately.

Exercise 2:
Fill in the appropriate word: *(for, his, her, leg, your).*

1. He had ______________ tonsils removed when he was very young.
2. The best remedy ______________ severe burns is cold water.
3. What do you mean, shake a ______________. If I go too fast, I'll probably break a bone and you can't just take an aspirin ______________ a broken leg.
4. With a gun in ______________ hand, a bag over ______________ shoulder and a mask covering ______________ face, anyone would have thought she was about to rob a bank.
5. Take that lipstick off ______________ lips. It looks awful.

about = gegen

Just a word slightly beside the point: As we said above, doctors are trying to do something about the horror of cancer. The same usage applies when we say, traffic engineers are trying to do something about the terrible traffic problems in our cities, *or,* what can the average citizen do about the destruction of our trees, *or,* I wish politicians would stop talking about pollution and do something about it.

Crime and Punishment

A murderer is a man who commits murder. A robber is a man who commits robbery. A blackmailer is a man who obtains an advantage or especially money often by threatening to reveal information that the other person would very much prefer to have kept confidential (= Erpresser). A shoplifter commits the crime of shoplifting, which means to steal from a shop *(Br. E.)* or store *(Am. E.)*

Murder is a capital crime, meaning punishable by death. Robbery is a serious offence, punishable by imprisonment, meaning you could go to gaol *(Br. E.)* or jail *(Am. E.;* the pronunciation of the two words is exactly the same) should

you be caught by the police. Some people think that shoplifting is a petty crime, meaning a minor one, but often it depends on the money value of the thing stolen.

If the police catch you stealing a diamond necklace, they will arrest you for sure.

If a court convicts you of robbery, the judge will probably sentence you to prison. The sentence might be for several years. In prison your fellow prisoners might call each other jailbirds *(Am. E.)* or gaolbirds *(Br. E.)*. Both kinds of English speakers might refer to each other as convicts, and after leaving prison they find it hard to live with the stigma of being an ex-convict or ex-con for short.

Vocabulary:

murderer = Mörder

commit (a crime, e.g. to commit a burglary) = eine Tat begehen (eine Sünde begehen = to commit a sin)

arrest = verhaften (He was arrested by the sheriff for murder.)

to convict = für schuldig erklären (He was convicted of kidnapping.)

a convict = Sträfling

A useful dictionary exercise might be to look up in a German-English dictionary some terms for crimes — many of those words are also used figuratively, e. g., rape (= vergewaltigen): chemicals which rape the earth, meaning which destroy the soil.

Examples:

A person is considered innocent until proven guilty. He could not prove he was innocent and was found guilty by the jury. The judge pronounced the sentence. The sentence was life imprisonment. He was sentenced to 30 days in jail for drunk driving. The judge said, "You should be put in prison for committing that crime. In fact, I wish the

prison guards would lock you up and throw away the keys!"
For certain types of crimes you will not be sent to prison, but you might receive a fine, or a monetary penalty (= Geldstrafe). Sometimes, people say, white-collar criminals get off too easy, meaning that white-collar crime is not punished hard enough. An example of white-collar crime is embezzlement (= Unterschlagung); fraud (= Betrug) or tax evasion (= Steuerhinterziehung) are other instances. The opposite of white-collar is blue-collar, but we do not usually speak of blue-collar crime. We usually say, though, blue-collar worker and white-collar worker to differentiate manual workers from office workers, i. e., people who work with their hands as opposed to those who have desk jobs.

"The judge sentenced him to 60 days in jail or a fine of $ 500."
"He was fined $ 100 for speeding" (= driving too fast in a car).

(→ A Miscellany of Confounded Words: rob/steal; lend/borrow, etc.)

By the way, what's a "Krimi"? Whether as a book or movie or TV show we say: detective story or mystery or sometimes murder mystery, for instance, when talking about Sherlock Holmes or the American writer Raymond Chandler, whose books were made into films — sometimes starring Humphrey Bogart. A thriller simply means exciting, or full of suspense, or maybe a spine tingling horror show like Frankenstein or Dracula.
Again, the word crime is used to mean Verbrechen. Murder is a crime, committed by a criminal. Crime does not pay, meaning that to violate the law, to commit a criminal offence is not worth it in the end. And, finally, the crime rate is increasing, and many people think we need more police officers to prevent crime.

Joke

Clyde: "What's the difference between: immoral and illegal?"
Hank: "I don't know."
Clyde: "Immoral is something wrong and 'ill eagle' is a sick bird!"

Adjectives
Comparison of Adjectives

Comparison of Adjectives

There are two ways of forming comparisons in English. You either add *-er/-est* to an adjective:

dark — darker — darkest

or you put the words *more/most* before the adjective:

beautiful — more beautiful — most beautiful.

Which form you use depends on the adjective:

One-syllable adjectives normally take the ending **-er/-est:**
tall — tall**er** — tall**est**
clean — clean**er** — clean**est.**

Adjectives of three syllables and more and participles form their comparison with **more/most:**
beautiful — **more** beautiful — **most** beautiful
characteristic — **more** characteristic — **most** characteristic
interesting — **more** interesting — **most** interesting
interested — **more** interested — **most** interested.

You will realize that the two-syllable adjectives are missing in the above rules. And indeed, while one-syllable and many-syllable adjectives follow the hard and fast rules given above, the two-syllable adjectives pose a certain problem insofar as some take *-er/-est,* others *more/most* and some admit even both forms. We have compiled a short list for you, which of course is far from being comprehensive. If you need more detailed information, we have to refer you to your grammar book. But you could perhaps complete the list with adjectives you come across in your texts.

-er/-est	more/most	both forms
funny	antique	common
friendly	bizarre	pleasant
wealthy	afraid	stupid, etc.
narrow	alive	
simple	alone	
noble	awful	
clever	aware	
mature, etc.	doubtful, etc.	

There is one more word to say about the use of *more.* If you compare two qualities of one and the same thing or person, you have to use *more:*
Examples: He is more mad than stupid.
This story is more sad than funny.
Here the word *more* corresponds to the German eher.

Comparison of Adjectives Exercise

By the way, the negative comparative forms are always *less* and *least* regardless of how many syllables an adjective has.
Examples: Jane is less nice than Susan. Mary was the least beautiful girl in the group.

Exercise 1:
Put the adjective in brackets into the comparative form like this:

John is (tall) than Mary. — John is taller than Mary.
He was (curious) than afraid.
— He was more curious than afraid.

1. I have never heard a (bizarre) story than yours.
2. When I gave him a dollar, he became much (friendly).
3. He never felt (alone) than in a crowd of people.
4. His mother seemed (worried) about the accident than he was.
5. Her youngest son was much (shy) than all her other children.
6. I think you have become (thin) since I last saw you.
7. It would have been (clever) to tell the truth right away.
8. The (simple) an explanation is, the better.
9. They became (quiet) and (quiet).
10. I was (dead) than alive.

Now let's tackle the next problem. Of course, there are some adjectives which do not have regular comparison forms, in other words, you have to learn a few exceptions. But you'll know most of them anyway.

good (gut) well (gesund)	— better	— best
bad (schlecht) ill (krank)	— worse	— worst
much many	— more	— most
little (klein)	— smaller	— smallest
little (wenig)	— less[1]	— least[1]
far	— farther	— farthest
far	— further	— furthest[2]
old	— older	— oldest
old	— elder	— eldest[3]

[1] As mentioned earlier the forms *less* and *least* are used to make a negative comparison.

[2] You use the forms *farther* and *farthest* for distance only. *Further* and *furthest* can be used for distance and figuratively.
I can't go any farther/further. Have you got any further questions?
As you can see from the examples, this is true for adjectives and adverbs.

[3] The forms *elder* and *eldest* are used for comparisions within the family, e. g.: my elder brother, his eldest son. But you cannot use these forms before *than:* My brother is older than I am.

Adjectives
Comparison of Adjectives

Before we go into the exercises, we would like to draw your attention to two pairs of adjectives which are easily confused:

next/nearest — last/latest

Look at the following examples:

Do you know where Burton Road is?	
— Yes, it's the *next* on the left.	Ja, die nächste Straße links.
Will you be at our *next* meeting?	. . . bei unserem nächsten Treffen?
Next Sunday is the 12th.	Der nächste Sonntag . . .
Where is the *nearest* bus stop?	. . . die nächste Bushaltestelle?

In German it's always nächste whereas in English you have to distinguish whether you talk about *distance* which means that you use *nearest,* or sequence which calls for *next.* (→ A Miscellany of Confounded Words, p. 15)

With last and latest it's a bit easier, because we can give you a  : The opposite of *last* is *first,* the opposite of *latest* is *earliest.* And the German for *latest* is often neueste.

The *last* letters of the alphabet are XYZ.	Die letzten Buchstaben . . .
He had spent his *last* dollar.	. . . seinen letzten Dollar.
Verdi's *last* opera was "Falstaff".	Verdis letzte Oper . . .
Have you heard the *latest* about the war?	. . . das Neueste . . .
the *latest* fashion	die neueste Mode
the very *latest* improvements	die allerneuesten Verbesserungen
But:	
at (the) latest	(aller)spätestens
Please be here tomorrow *at the latest.*	

Comparison of Adjectives Exercise

Exercise 2:
Find the missing words — they are all irregular comparative forms — and enter them in the boxes of the word puzzle. If you have chosen the right words, you will get a hidden phrase which fits into sentence 10.

1. Can you tell me where the __________ bank is, please?
2. Enclosed please find our __________ order before we go on holiday.
3. For __________ information please contact our local sales representative.
4. She is wearing the __________ in hats.
5. It's not a bad mark, but it's __________ than your usual one.
6. He didn't feel well yesterday, but he is __________ today.
7. Look! This is our little cottage. It looks __________ than it really is.
8. I've got little spare time at the moment and I will have even __________ when I start my new job.
9. If this bank is closed, you have to go to the __________.
10. She was __________ yesterday evening and kept us all amused.

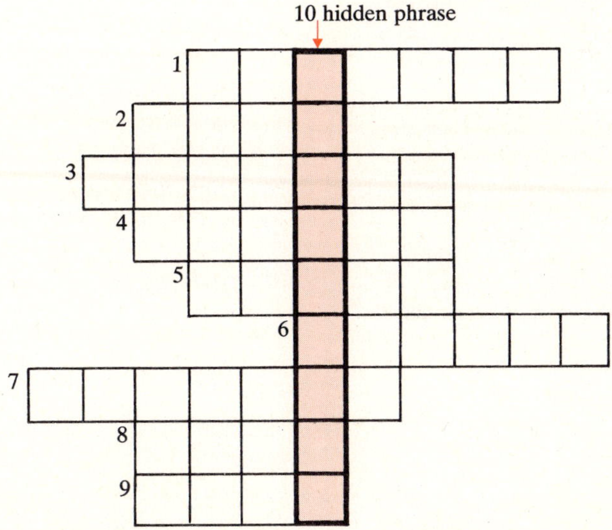

Adjectives
Constructions with Comparisons

Exercise 3:
Put in *elder, older, eldest* or *oldest.*

1. All her children are married except for her __________ daughter.
2. My brother is __________ than I am, but only by one year.
3. His __________ sister is called Mary.
4. This is our __________ church. It was built in the twelfth century.
5. His two sons look the same age. Which is the __________?

Constructions with Comparisons

1. The Positive Form
If you want to express that two things are equally good, bad, big, etc., or not equally good, bad, big, etc., you say:

His English is *as good as* his French.

He is *not* $\left\{\begin{matrix} \textit{so} \\ \textit{as} \end{matrix}\right\}$ *old as* I am.

Riding a horse is *not* $\left\{\begin{matrix} \textit{so} \\ \textit{as} \end{matrix}\right\}$ *easy as* riding a bicycle.

Exercise 4:
Combine the two sentences like this:
John is tall. So is Bob. = John is *as tall as* Bob.

1. Russian is difficult. So is Greek.
2. Your coffee is good. So is my mother's coffee.
3. Teachers work hard. So do students.
4. Cats are intelligent. So are dogs.
5. Our living room is large. So is our bedroom.
6. Skiing is strenuous fun. So is skating.

Exercise 5:
Take the sentences from exercise 4 and combine them into a negative comparison like this:

John is *not* $\left\{\begin{matrix} \textit{so} \\ \textit{as} \end{matrix}\right\}$ *tall as* Bob.

Constructions with Comparisons
Positive Form/Comparative Form

Exercise 6:

We have collected a few idioms of comparison for you, e. g.,
as busy as a bee = bienenfleißig.
Do you think you can match the English idioms with their German equivalents?

1. as blind as a bat	A eiskalt
2. as bold as brass	B stockblind
3. as clear as crystal	C mausetot
4. as cold as charity	D stocktaub
5. as dead as a doornail	E kristallklar, sonnenklar
6. as deaf as a post	F kerngesund
7. as easy as pie (anything)	G treu wie Gold
8. as fit as a fiddle	H kinderleicht
9. as light as a feather	I frech wie Oskar
10. as mad as a hatter (March hare)	J blitzschnell
11. as quick as lightning	K federleicht
12. as true as steel	L total übergeschnappt

It's 1. B, ______________________________

2. The Comparative Form

If you want to say that something is better, worse, bigger, you use the following construction:

His English is *better than* mine.
He is *more intelligent than* you are.
She is *less pretty than* her sister.
Riding a horse is *more difficult than* riding a bicycle.

Exercise 7:

Make sentences:
e. g. Gold/expensive/silver/because/it/rare.
Gold is *more expensive than* silver, because it is rarer.

1. He/good/his brother/because/he/careful.
2. A Mercedes/fast/Fiat/because/the engine/big.
3. Summer/nice/winter/because/it/warm.
4. Robert/successful/Peter/because/he/works hard

Adjectives
Comparatives and Superlatives

There are two other instances where you use this form:

The bigger the house, *the more* money it will cost.	Je größer das Haus, desto mehr Geld kostet es.
It is getting *colder and colder.*	Es wird immer kälter.

Exercise 8:

Put in a suitable comparative form.

e. g.: The more you earn, ________ taxes you have to pay.

The more you earn, the more taxes you have to pay.

1. The cheaper you buy goods, ________________ you can sell them.
2. The more energy you waste, ________________ is left for following generations.
3. The higher up you get, ________________ the air becomes.
4. The more you learn, ________________ you know.

Exercise 9:

Put in *as, than* or *and.*

1. He is only twelve, but already ______ tall ______ his mother.
   But he is still much shorter ______ his father.
2. The more he read of the story, the more ______ more interested he became.
3. Have you ever seen anything more beautiful ______ this rose?
4. Please let us have your catalogue ______ soon ______ possible.
5. I was more angry ______ frightened.
6. It was getting warmer ______ warmer.
7. He was less polite ______ he used to be.

Adjectives Used as Nouns
Abstract Adjectives

3. The Superlative Form

When you compare three or more persons or things you say:

> Tom is *the cleverest* boy in the class,
> but he isn't the *most diligent* one.

Exercise 10:

Answer the following questions by using the adjective *in italics* in its superlative form.

e. g.: Is London a *beautiful* town?
Yes, it's *the most beautiful* town I have ever seen.

Instead of *I have ever seen* you may have to use *I have ever met/heard,* etc., depending on the context.

1. Is Mrs. Brown a *nice* woman? — Yes, ______
2. Is John a *good* student? — Yes, ______
3. Was it a *bad* accident you had? ______
4. Is your dog *intelligent?* ______
5. Was the play *interesting?* ______
6. Did you really say the concert was *terrible?* ______

Adjectives Used as Nouns

1. Abstract Adjectives

In general, an English adjective cannot be used as a noun as freely as in German. There are however cases where they can be used as nouns. Look at the following examples:

They ventured into the unknown	Sie wagten sich ins Unbekannte.
They often prefer the old to the new.	Sie ziehen oft das Alte dem Neuen vor.
Hope for the best and expect the worst.	Hoffe das Beste und erwarte das Schlimmste.

Adjectives

Adjectives Used as Nouns

Here the adjectives are used in a general sense. As soon as you put them in a more specific context, you need a noun like *thing, matter, element,* etc., to “support” the adjective:

Das Seltsame daran war, . . .	The *strange thing* about it was . . .
Das Außerordentliche dieses Romans wurde sofort erkannt.	The *exceptional quality* of this novel was recognized immediately.
Das Komische in seinen Stücken . . .	The *comic element* in his plays . . .

2. Adjectives Used as Plural Nouns

The old often resist change.	Die Alten wehren sich oft gegen Veränderung.
The rich will help *the poor.*	Die Reichen werden den Armen helfen.
The wise look to the wiser for advice.	Die Weisen wenden sich an die Weiseren um Rat.
After the battle they buried *the dead.*	Nach der Schlacht begruben sie die Toten.

In the above examples, the adjectives have a plural meaning and thus they are followed by a plural verb. If you want to denote a single person, you must add a noun like *man, woman, person,* etc.

Der Alte bekam eine gute Pension.	The *old man* received a good pension.
Der Kranke wird oft ungeduldig, wenn . . .	The *sick person* often gets impatient if . . .
Nun ist der große Einsame ganz allein.	Now the *great solitary man* is quite alone.
Eine Achtzehnjährige starb, weil . . .	An *eighteen-year-old girl* died because . . .

Exercise 11:

Look at the sentences below. If necessary, add one of the following words: *element, man, thing, topics, woman.*

1. The extremely old ______________ need a great deal of attention.
2. The old ______________ who died in the accident yesterday has not yet been identified.

3. We will nurse your sick ________________ and feed your hungry ________________.
4. The sick ________________ had to be taken to hospital where he was operated at once.
5. They spoke about the most banal ________________.
6. The important ________________ is that you don't overexert yourself when doing this sort of physical exercise.
7. The young ________________ in spirit enjoy life.
8. You have to take the bad ________________ with the good ________________.
9. I enjoy the tragic ________________ in his novels.

3. *One* as a Substitute

As you have seen in the chapters above, an adjective normally needs a noun to accompany it. Adjectives can, however, be used without their nouns if the noun is replaced by the word *one* (singular) or *ones* (plural).

> My *cheap camera* seems to be just as good as your *expensive one.*
> If we compare *British universities* with *American ones* . . .

Unfortunately there is no rule without exception. You do not use the "prop-word" *one* after

own:	I won't need your car, I can take my own.
following:	We have to ask you some questions. Please answer the following.
one, two, three, etc.:	I'd like to book two seats to New York and one to Montreal.

One is sometimes omitted after !

the + comparative:	The police first searched the larger room and then the smaller (one).
the + superlative:	I took the largest (one).
adjectives of colour:	I want the blue (one).

Adjectives
Adjectives Used as Nouns

Exercise 12:

Put in *one* or *ones* where necessary.

1. I think I'll sell my old car and buy a new ___________.
2. Is this house your own ___________ or have you just rented it?
3. I want some tickets for tonight's performance, but not such expensive ___________.
4. If you had the choice, would you take the bigger or the smaller ___________?
5. Which dress do you like better? The red ___________ or the blue ___________.
6. Small bananas are often better than big ___________.
7. I need some information. Could you tell me the following ___________?

Jokes

Question: What is black and white and has 16 wheels?
Answer: A zebra on roller skates.

Question: When are cooks mean?
Answer: When they beat the eggs and whip the cream.

Question: What is a three-letter word for mousetrap?
Answer: CAT.

Trip, Stumble, Fall
False Friends

False friends — faux amis — falsche Freunde — false cognates

False friends are words which exist in English and in German and therefore look as if they were good friends, because they have exactly or almost the same form in both languages. They are, however, *false friends* because they differ completely or partly in meaning!

Look at the following example of a typical false friend:

Eventually he'll be successful

Try to translate this sentence or to find a synonym for *eventually*.
Well, eventually means finally, in the end = schließlich, endlich, eines Tages, so the sentence means: Eines Tages wird er Erfolg haben. As you can see, it does not mean eventuell, which may be translated by *perhaps* for example.

Now study the following list of false friends. When you go through it, cover the right side and try to find the translations yourself before you look at the solutions.

1. action ['ækʃn] ≠ Aktion

action = Handeln, Tat
We must take action at once. — Wir müssen sofort handeln.
Actions are more important than words. — Taten sind wichtiger als Worte.
Aktion = campaign, drive, operation
Alle seine politischen Aktionen erwiesen sich als Fehlschläge. — All his political campaigns/operations turned out to be a failure.

2. actual ['æktʃuəl] ≠ aktuell

actual(ly) = wirklich, tatsächlich, eigentlich
The actual number of addicts is higher than police statistics show. — Die tatsächliche Zahl der Drogenabhängigen ist größer als die Polizeistatistik angibt.

Trip, Stumble, Fall
False Friends

Did you actually see the Queen in person?	Hast du wirklich die Queen selbst gesehen?
aktuell	= topical, current, relevant, up-to-date, in fashion
ein aktuelles Thema	an issue of topical importance
die aktuelle Mode	current fashion
Miniröcke sind wieder aktuell.	Mini skirts are in fashion again.

3. alley ['ælɪ] ≠ Allee

alley	= Gasse
Allee	= avenue, boulevard

4. ambulance ['æmbjʊləns] ≠ Ambulanz

ambulance	= Krankenwagen
Ambulanz	= 1. outpatients' department; emergency ward (2. ambulance)

5. artist ['a:tɪst] ≠ Artist

artist	= Künstler
Artist	= circus performer; variety-artist

6. become [bɪ'kʌm] ≠ bekommen

become	= werden
He was to become one of the most distinguished artists of his age.	Er sollte einer der hervorragendsten Künstler seiner Zeit werden.
bekommen	= get, receive
Er bekam, was er wollte.	He got what he wanted.

7. blame [bleɪm] ≠ blamieren

→ A Micellany of Confounded Words, p. 9

8. career [kə'rɪə] ≠ Karriere

career	= 1. Beruf(slaufbahn)
I think all careers should be open to women nowadays.	Ich finde, heute sollten den Frauen alle Berufe offenstehen.
	2. Karriere

9. chef [ʃef] ≠ Chef

chef	= Küchenchef, Chefkoch
Chef	= boss, head
Er ist mein Chef	He's my boss (not ✗ he's my chief ✗)
chief (noun)	= Oberhaupt, Häuptling

chief of State	Staatsoberhaupt
chief (adjective)	= Ober-, Chef-
chief inspector	Ober-, Chefinspector

10. Christ [kraɪst], **Christendom** ['krɪsəndəm] ≠ Christ, Christentum

Christ	= Christus
Christendom	= Christenheit
Christ	= Christian
Christentum	= Christianity

11. concept ['kɒnsept] ≠ Konzept

concept	= Begriff
Konzept	= 1. draft, notes
das Konzept eines Briefes	the draft of a letter
ohne Konzept sprechen	to speak without notes
	2. programme (= *Br. E.;* program = *Am. E.)*
Die Partei hat kein klares bildungspolitisches Konzept.	The party doesn't have a clear-cut programme of educational policy.

Trip, Stumble, Fall
False Friends

12. concern [kən'sɛːn] ≠ Konzern

concern = 1. Anliegen, Sorge

Money was his only concern. — Seine einzige Sorge galt dem Geld.

Your problems are not my concern. — Deine Probleme sind nicht meine Sorge.

2. Unternehmen, Betrieb

Our concern produces office furniture only. — Unser Betrieb stellt nur Büromöbel her.

Konzern = group of companies

Ein Konzern besteht aus einer Muttergesellschaft und einer oder mehreren Tochtergesellschaften. — A group of companies consists of a parent company and one or more subsidiaries.

13. confession [kən'feʃn] ≠ Konfession

confession = Geständnis, Beichte

Konfession = denomination

14. consequent ['kɒnsɪkwənt] ≠ konsequent

consequent(ly) = folglich, folgend

The rain was heavy — and consequently the land was flooded. — Es gab schwere Regenfälle und folglich/daraufhin wurde das Land überschwemmt.

konsequent = consistent, systematic

Sie sollten Ihren Kindern gegenüber konsequent sein. — You should be consistent with your children.

15. control [kən'troul] ≠ kontrollieren

→ A Miscellany of Confounded Words, p. 12

16. critic ['krɪtɪk] ≠ Kritik

critic = Kritiker

Kritik = critique, criticism, review

In seiner Kritik lobte er vor allem die Schauspieler. — In his critique he praised above all the actors.

eine Film-/Buchkritik — the review of a film/book

Seine scharfe Kritik an ihrem Benehmen brachte sie zum Weinen. — His sharp criticism of her behaviour made her cry.

17. decent ['di:snt] ≠ dezent

decent	= anständig
He's a decent fellow.	Er ist ein anständiger Kerl.
a decent meal	ein anständiges Essen
dezent	= discreet, unobtrusive, soft
dezentes Parfüm	discreet perfume
dezente Musik	soft music
ein dezentes Rot	an unobtrusive shade of red

18. delicate ['delɪkət] ≠ delikat

delicate	= zart, fein
He was a delicate child.	Er war ein zartes Kind.
delikat	delicious

19. disinterested [dɪs'ɪntrəstɪd] ≠ desinteressiert

disinterested	= uneigennützig
His decision was not altogether disinterested.	Seine Entscheidung war nicht ganz uneigennützig.
desinteressiert	= uninterested
Sie war an ihrer Arbeit völlig desinteressiert.	She was completely uninterested in her work.

20. eventual [ɪ'ventʃuəl] ≠ eventuell

eventual(ly)	= schließlich, endlich, eines Tages, am Ende
He worked so hard that he eventually made himself ill.	Er arbeitete so schwer, daß er sich schließlich krank machte.
Eventually, Hansel and Gretel find their way home.	Am Ende finden Hänsel und Gretel den Weg nach Hause.
eventuell	= perhaps, possible/possibly, may, might
Er kommt eventuell morgen.	He may/might come tomorrow./ Perhaps he'll come tomorrow.

21. fatal ['feɪtl] ≠ fatal

fatal	= tödlich
a fatal accident	ein tödlicher Unfall
fatal	= 1. awkward, embarrassing

Trip, Stumble, Fall
False Friends

Wir befanden uns in einer fatalen Lage. — We were in an awkward (embarrassing) position.

2. disastrous

Das war ein fataler Irrtum! — That was a disastrous error!

22. fraction ['frækʃn] ≠ Fraktion

fraction = Bruch(teil)

Fraktion = parliamentary group/party

23. genial ['dʒi:njəl] ≠ genial

genial = freundlich, herzlich

She greeted me with a genial smile. — Sie begrüßte mich mit einem herzlichen Lächeln.

genial = ingenious

eine geniale Idee — an ingenious idea

24. gymnasium [dʒɪm'neɪzjəm] ≠ Gymnasium

gymnasium = Turnhalle

Gymnasium = *Br. E.:* grammar school; *Am. E.:* high school, secondary school.

25. human ['hju:mən] ≠ human

human = menschlich, Menschen-. . .

the human body — der menschliche Körper

a human life — ein Menschenleben

Human means belonging to or concerning man and is the opposite of animal.

human = humane [hju'mein]

eine humane Behandlung unserer Gefangenen — a humane treatment of our convicts

aus humanen Gründen — for reasons of humanity

(Tierschutzverein = *Am. E.* Humane Society)

26. menu ['menju:] ≠ Menü

menu = Speisekarte

Menü = set meal/dinner/lunch

Menü 2 bitte! — Dinner 2, please!

False Friends Exercise

27. murder ['mɛːdə] ≠ Mörder

murder = Mord
Mörder = murderer
(→ Crime and Punishment, p. 48)

28. overhear [ˌəuvəˈhɪə] ≠ überhören

overhear = (zufällig) mithören
They didn't know that I had overheard their talk. — Sie wußten nicht, daß ich ihr Gespräch mitgehört hatte.
überhören = not to hear; ignore
Ich habe das Klingeln überhört. Was ihm nicht paßt, überhört er einfach. — I didn't hear the bell. He simply ignores what he doesn't like.

29. pension ['penʃn] ≠ Pension

pension = Rente, Pension
Pension 1. Hotel = boardinghouse, guesthouse, pension (not in English-speaking countries, only in continental Europe)
2. Ruhestand = retirement
in Pension gehen — to retire

30. photograph ['fəutəgrɑːf] ≠ Fotograf

photograph = Fotografie
Fotograf = photographer [fəˈtɒgrəfə^r]

31. principal ['prɪnsəpl] ≠ prinzipiell

principal = hauptsächlich, Haupt-. . .
his principal occupation — seine Hauptbeschäftigung
prinzipiell = of/on/in principle
eine prinzipielle Frage — a question of principle
Prinzipiell bin ich einverstanden, aber . . . — In principle I agree, but . . .
Das tue ich prinzipiell nicht. — On principle I don't do that.

Trip, Stumble, Fall
False Friends

---

32. prospect ['prɒspekt] ≠ Prospekt

prospect	= Aussicht
Prospekt	= prospectus, leaflet, brochure

33. self-conscious [ˌself'kɒnʃəs] ≠ selbstbewußt

self-conscious	= befangen, gehemmt
She was too self-conscious to go out alone.	Sie war zu gehemmt, alleine auszugehen.
selbstbewußt	= self-confident

34. sensible ['sensəbl] ≠ sensibel

sensible	= vernünftig
a sensible solution	eine vernünftige Lösung
sensibel	= sensitive
ein sensibles Kind	a sensitive child

35. serious ['sɪərɪəs] ≠ seriös

serious	= ernst(haft)
seriös	= respectable
ein seriöser Mann	a respectable man
eine seriöse Firma	a firm of good standing

36. spare [speə] ≠ sparen

→ The Language of Money, Money, p. 84

37. stream [stri:m] ≠ Strom

stream	= Bach
Strom	= river

38. sympathetic [ˌsɪmpə'θetɪk] ≠ sympathisch

sympathetic	= mitfühlend
She was a most sympathetic woman.	Sie war eine äußerst mitfühlende Frau.
sympathisch	= likable
ein sympathischer Mensch	a likable person

False Friends Exercise

39. technique [tek'ni:k] ≠ Technik
→ A Miscellany of Confounded Words, p. 19

40. warehouse ['weəhaus] ≠ Warenhaus
→ A Miscellany of Confounded Words, p. 20

Exercise
Put the German word in brackets into its proper English form.

1. XYZ Ltd. started a ________________ (Werbeaktion) to launch their new product.
2. The trade unions were confronted with the ________________ (aktuell) problem of young people not wanting to become members.
3. An ________________ (Allee) of poplars led up to the house.
4. After his accident he was taken to the ________________ (Ambulanz) of the nearest hospital.
5. He wanted to become a ________________ (Artist), but his parents were very much against it.
6. He finally ________________ (werden) a famous ________________ (Künstler).
7. He ________________ (bekam) the best education possible at that time.
8. He decided to become a ________________ (Berufs-)diplomat.
9. My ________________ (Chef) always calls me at 8 o'clock to check if I am on time.
10. He was a born-again ________________ (Christ), and ________________ (Christentum) seemed to him the only possible form of religion.
11. Although he gave the lecture for the first time, he spoke without ________________ (Konzept).

Trip, Stumble, Fall
False Friends

12. Nowadays even big ________________ (Konzerne) suffer from the world-wide recession.
13. I know that you are a Christian, but which ________________ (Konfession) do you belong to?
14. You can either use British or American spelling, only be ________________ (konsequent).
15. In his ________________ (Kritik) of the new play, the ________________ (Kritiker) praised the acting but criticized the bland lighting and sets. A ________________ (Kritik) of a book or film or play is simply the more popular term for critique.
16. The music and the lighting were ________________ (dezent) and the walls were decorated with ________________ (dezent) ornaments.
17. The meal was ________________ (delikat).
18. He is the most ________________ (desinteressiert) person I have ever met in all my life!
19. There are not many people who act in a completely ________________ (uneigennützig) way.
20. My sister who lives in Toronto will ________________ (eventuell) come to see me next summer.
21. The situation was becoming more and more ________________ (fatal).
22. In the German Bundestag there are now four ________________ (Fraktionen).
23. I think the pocket calculator is an ________________ (genial) invention, especially for people like me who are bad at doing calculations.
24. After primary school he went to ________________ (Gymnasium).
25. Is the treatment of our prisoners really ________________ (human) enough?

False Friends Exercise

26. They served a wonderful ________________ (Menü).
27. In former times ________________ (Mörder) were hanged.
    He was tried for ________________ (Mord).
28. I think he ________________ (hat überhört) what you said.
29. As I don't like big hotels, I was looking for a nice, quiet ________________ (Pension).
30. I am a very bad ________________ (Fotograf).
31. He is an extremely puritan person and doesn't go to the cinema ________________ (prinzipiell = aus Prinzip).
    Well, ________________ (prinzipiell = im Prinzip) I would refuse such an offer, but in your case I'll accept.
32. We are enclosing a ________________ (Prospekt) of our products and hope you will find this information useful.
33. Learning judo had turned the once shy girl into a ________________ (selbstbewußt) woman.
34. You know, she always says she is very ________________ (sensibel), but she never seems to realize when other people suffer.
35. We should only invite ________________ (seriöse) customers to our erotic art auction.
36. Even at the age of 83, my aunt remembered the seven most important ________________ (Ströme) of Africa — a piece of extremely useless information for an old lady.
37. She was the most ________________ (sympathisch) person I had ever known and very sympathetic towards everyone who was in trouble.

Discrimination and Prejudice

Whether writing about the Middle East conflict, the generation gap, the race problem in America, or the foreign workers in Europe, again and again the subject of discrimination and prejudice

arises. Often, it is a question of minorities — Jews or political refugees, Mediterranean people living and working in Northern Europe, the mentally ill or unemployed — facing a majority of fellow human beings who have already formed an image of what these "others" are like.

If you make a judgement about someone before actually meeting them or knowing them, if you pre-judge others based on what you have heard or read about them, that is what is meant by *prejudice,* a word quite similar in usage and meaning to the German word Vorurteil.

The words *discriminate* and *discrimination* are probably so often used incorrectly because in English they have two sets of meaning and hence two different usages.
The first meaning of discriminate is to distinguish or differentiate, to be able to tell what is best. In this sense it corresponds to the German unterscheiden, e. g.:
He can discriminate between French and Italian wines by tasting them.
So a discriminating person is not usually negative at all, but means someone who has refined taste, can choose the best thing.
The meaning we are most concerned with is equivalent to the German sense of diskriminieren = herabsetzen, benachteiligen, and in English, then, we must use the modifier *against,* e. g.:
South African law discriminates against Black Africans. Discrimination against female workers should stop.
Prejudice is often used with *against,* but not always: She is prejudiced against jobless persons; she thinks everyone can find a job.
The way to form the opposite is with *in favour of (= Br. E.;* favor = *Am. E.),* e. g.:
To discriminate in favour of family members; to be prejudiced in favour of young people. There is, in some countries, discrimination in favour of fat people.
In German you would have to use words like begünstigen, bevorzugen/Begünstigung, Bevorzugung.

Notice, discrimination has no plural (→ Mass Nouns, p. 35).
We say, e. g.:
There is a lot of discrimination against old people in Western countries.
Just as we say, e. g.:

Discrimination and Prejudice Exercise

There is too much prejudice against rock 'n' roll.
But we can form a plural of prejudice and say, e. g.:
He has a number of prejudices about families with very many children. I have heard people express various prejudices against Gipsies (= *Br. E.;* Gipsies = *Am. E.)* (= Sinti or Zigeuner). Some dictionaries do not even capitalize the name of this people. Do you have any prejudices?

Exercise 1:
Fill in *against, about, discrimination, discriminated, prejudice, prejudices.* Use each word only once.

Jonathan Swift (1667—1745), a satirist, was born in Ireland. In his works he attacked many ________________. In *Modest Proposal* he wrote bitter prose striking at those who ________________ ________________ the Irish poor. In *Gulliver's Travels* his satire was directed against political and nationalistic ________________ and its results. He once set down an essay ridiculing ________________ ________________ servants and maids.

As a result of growing self-awareness and self-confidence, minorities in the United States have staged various forms of protest against prejudice and discrimination. One could consider these protests as an outcry against the "melting pot" — on the one hand because in reality this American ideal of integration never worked and on the other hand because ethnic minorities no longer believe that "Americanization" is a desirable or necessary goal, particularly if that means giving up all ties to one's ancestral soil (→ The Plain Truth . . ., p. 134) or roots. None of these movements are out to praise ghetto life. Bussing — the practice of driving school children long distances to integrate them in schools outside of their segregated neighbourhoods (= *Br. E.;* neighborhoods = *Am. E.)* — was a measure imposed by the courts to achieve long-term integration, but was never well-received by those affected.

— de jure segregation = supported by law, as in South Africa
— de facto segregation = non-integration because of racial separation in residential neighborhoods

If Americans agree on wanting to integrate in principle, there seems to be an increasing desire to promote ethnic culture and traditions. Certainly, this stems in part from disillusions and loss of pride Americans have suffered over the last twenty years. Ethnic groups are tired of the feeling of being oppressed by the

Discrimination and Prejudice
Exercises

WASP (White Anglo-Saxon Protestant = the dominant culture in the U.S.A.) majority.
— oppressed = to be ruled in a hard or cruel way (to live under oppression)
— suppressed = to put down or crush by forceful means (to suppress a rebellion)
— repress = verdrängen; to hold away from view (a psychological term)

Ethnic groups are not quite the same as racial groups. As yet there have been no press reports about ethnic riots or ethnic violence. England and America have seen race riots, though. Race = Rasse.
— racialism = discrimination against races; belief that the races are different
— racism = a stronger form of prejudice which believes in a superior race

Some of the larger ethnic groups in the U.S.A. are: German-Americans, Italian-Americans, Irish-Americans, Hispanic-Americans or Hispanics.

Exercise 2:
HIDDEN WORD PUZZLE
(Not all these words appear in the text!)

a person who has a negative image of other peoples or races
unreasoned bias against persons
a person in need who asks for money
to select carefully
to fight against the established or traditional
a preposition, opposite of *for*
to strike against or provoke severely
opposite of love
a person owned as property

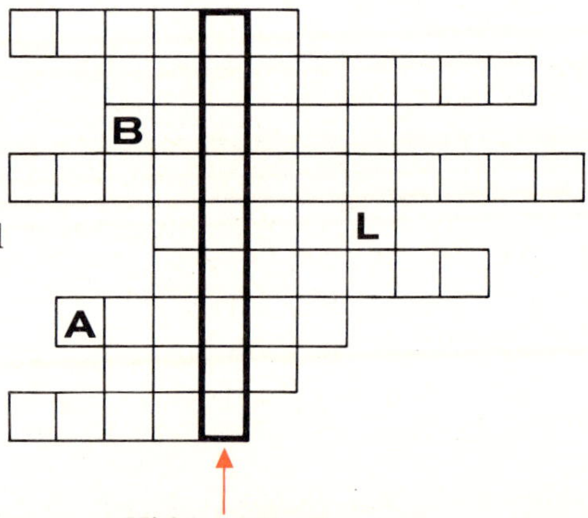

Hidden Word

Discrimination and Prejudice Puzzle Exercises

Exercise 3:

CROSSWORD PUZZLE
(Not all these words appear in the text!)

ACROSS:

1. foreigner, from another country or planet
2. preposition, opposite of *on*
3. car
4. preposition, *in* or *around*
5. abbreviation of road
6. black people (pl.)
7. s.o. who betrays his country or people
8. pronoun, 3rd person singular, neuter
9. pronoun, 3rd person singular, feminine
10. 3rd person singular present tense of the verb *go*
11. possessive pronoun, 1st person plural

DOWN:

1. preposition with discriminate (opposite of *in favor [Br. E. favour] of)*
2. an illegal or out-of-control demonstration
3. to join
4. synonym for *thus*
5. opposite of *yes*
6. family background or ancestors
7. to lose color (*Br. E.* colour)
8. exclamation of surprise
9. back part of a ship
10. pressure that worries

Gerunds = -ing forms

Students often have trouble understanding and translating gerunds. We cannot deal with those problems here, but, perhaps, the following will help indirectly with the difficulties involved.
Students' written work rarely has mistakes connected with gerunds because they rarely attempt to produce gerunds. In fact, gerunds are ignored. Sometimes, though, certain constructions are attempted in written English that require gerunds and no other form. In this section we are going to talk about words and phrases which often need to be completed by the use of gerunds.
The most common error of this type is using the infinitive instead of the gerund.

A taboo example: ✗ He succeeded to pass the English test. ✗
corrected: He succeeded in passing the English test.

2nd taboo example: ✗ I enjoy to listen to classical music. ✗
corrected: I enjoy listening to classical music.

The first example is a case of a verb having a fixed preposition, e. g., to succeed in, which must be followed by a gerund. Here is another example which does not take the infinitive:

interested in: She was interested in taking piano lessons.
They are interested in learning more about the United States.

(Of course, one could also say:
She was interested in piano lessons.
They are interested in the United States.)

We can already conclude from the above:

1. The fixed preposition after certain verbs is necessary whether or not we use a gerund.
2. The function of a gerund is usually to emphasize an activity — another name for a gerund is a verbal noun.
3. The rule of gerund after verbs with fixed prepositions only means that when choosing between infinitive and gerund one must use the gerund form.
After verb + fixed preposition one can also, of course, have a noun.

Gerund after Verb + Preposition

Sometimes one has difficulty in deciding whether *to* is a preposition or part of the infinitive. You can test this by asking yourself if *to* could be followed by a noun: I look forward to Christmas/to your visit. I look forward to seeing you. The rule is: If it can be followed by a noun, then the verbal form is with a gerund!

Let's take a look at some of the more common combinations of verb + preposition:

accuse of = beschuldigen/anklagen wegen	involved in = engagiert für
to be accustomed/used to = gewöhnt sein an	keep on (working) = weiter (arbeiten)
count on / depend on / rely on } sich verlassen/zählen auf	look forward to = sich freuen auf
give up = aufgeben	proud of = stolz auf
have difficulty with (in) = Schwierigkeiten haben mit (bei)	start up = anfangen
insist on = bestehen auf	succeed in = Erfolg haben bei/mit
interested in = interessiert an	talk about = sprechen über
	vote for = stimmen für
	to be worried about = sich Sorgen machen über

Now study the following examples carefully:

The agency was accused of leaking secrets to the press.

I am accustomed to drinking water with my meals. I hope I can get used to drinking beer.
You can count on my helping with the children.
The Johnsons had to depend on receiving financial aid from the State.
We relied on being able to find our own way *without asking* *) for help from anyone.

I gave up drinking beer with lunch and started losing weight fast.
The class insisted on having translations for every phrase they read.
It was not that she was not interested in buying the shoes, she had simply forgotten to bring enough money.

Gerunds = -ing forms

He was involved in dealing drugs.

Keep on trying, you'll learn it!

Let me just say, I look forward to meeting you with great pleasure.

Wendy was proud of earning so much money for just one evening's work.

I want to start up playing squash again — racquet ball ruined my stroke.

Elmer, the mechanic, succeeded in repairing the brakes in only half an hour.

The politicians talked about solving the unemployment catastrophe.

I voted for lowering taxes, but in the end the government did just the opposite.

They are all worried about losing their jobs.

*) -ing forms after prepositions alone:
e. g., After waiting for an hour, he left.

Before beginning the test, please read all the questions through.

Do you think you can go through the list above and make some sentences of your own?

Just try writing down a few of them and perhaps do some more later. O.K.? O.K.

I am proud of having ______________________________.

She was interested ______________________________.

We look ______________________________.

They are fond of ______________________________.

Phrases Requiring Gerunds Exercise

Another set of "required" gerunds is classified as *phrases with -ing forms.* This set is not as open-ended as the one before; here are almost all of them:

cannot help
cannot stand
cannot bear
it is no use, there is no use
it is no good
it is not worth
do you mind, would you mind

Again, look through these example sentences carefully:

I cannot help thinking the author lost track of what he wanted to say.

Our teacher cannot stand cheating on tests. She says it is not fair to the others.

I cannot bear this complaining any longer.

It's no use crying over spilled milk. (Old saying)

There's no use telling him about responsibility. He just won't understand.

It's no good punishing the children of foreign workers for the economic troubles.

It's not worth discussing. If I thought it was worth debating, I'd do so.

Do you mind finishing that later? No, it's not important.

Would you mind opening the wine bottle for me? No, I've had lots of practice.

(NOTICE: the answer to this request is "No" — I do not mind finishing, "No" — I would not mind opening the wine bottle. = Ich hätte nichts dagegen.)

Exercise 1:

Answer these questions, writing in the gerund forms:

Example: Would you mind closing the window?

No, I wouldn't mind closing it.

1. Is there any use writing to your Congressman? ____________________
____

2. Is it any good telling her about it? ____
____
____

3. Would you mind repeating that? ____
____
____

4. Was it worth getting into an argument? ____________________
____
____

Gerunds = -ing forms

5. Do you mind my sitting here? ______

______

______

6. Can you stand listening to that music when it's so loud? ______

______

______

7. I suppose you can't help always knowing the answer? ______

______

______

8. Can you bear hearing some more bad news? ______

______

______

These verbs require gerunds and not infinitives:

admit	finish
avoid	forgive
deny	imagine
dislike	postpone
enjoy	prevent
escape	resist
excuse	risk
suggest	

Again, look carefully at these examples:
He had to admit (that) finding a job was not very easy. He admitted (to) stealing.
We all want to avoid making silly mistakes.
If you deny having resisted arrest, the police will charge you with something else.
You shouldn't become a medical doctor if you dislike seeing blood.
I thoroughly enjoyed listening to Randy Newman's record. He's so witty.
He escaped going into the army, but had trouble later trying to find a job.
Please excuse my arriving so late for dinner.
I wish you hadn't finished eating so soon, I would have liked to have stayed longer.
Do forgive my bringing so few presents for the children. Forgive me for forgetting.

Just imagine having to work 48 hours a week and only getting one week paid vacation.
Let's postpone meeting the Ralstons till next week.
If only we could prevent them (from) building so many missiles, we'd have money to burn.
He can't resist making ironic comments.
I can't risk investing that much money in your miserable business.
Scientists suggest eating properly is the best medicine. And don't forget exercise.

Obligatory Gerunds

Let's look at a few gerunds in action:

Writing English means paying attention to the time and orientation point of the speaker. If you are tired of working on tenses, just wait until you see all the difficulties in learning prepositions. Expecting to achieve mastery of the English verbs you might feel like Sisyphus pushing a heavy rock up a hill.
Can you spot the 5 gerunds?*)
The two that begin sentences are a stylistic variation which could be replaced by infinitive forms. But, perhaps, your feeling will tell you that 'To expect to achieve . . .' is not as elegant.

We want to concentrate, though, on those gerunds that are "obligatory".

One such case is the verb *to mean,* which, in its sense of defining, is always followed by a gerund, e. g.: Becoming an Olympic athlete means training hard and cutting down on beer.

The verb *to mean* belongs in a category of verbs that take either the infinitive + to or a gerund. When to use infinitive or gerund is determined by the intention or meaning of the construction.

Some other verbs are:

remember	She remembers buying the present, but can't remember putting it in a sack.
stop	They stopped smoking because they knew smoking was bad for their health.
try	He tried making a daily list of things to do.
forget	He completely forgot making appointments and dates.

As with other -ing forms in English (→ p. 93), the -ing form in the gerund stresses that the English-speaking person is emphasizing the activity — movement, something happening — in what is related.

When I say, "I remembered to buy the present." I mean I did not forget, and, probably, I am not thinking of the event of buying but that I now have the present.
If I stop working, or if I stop drinking I am thinking about what I was doing when I stopped. The infinitive + to: I stopped to work, or I stopped to drink means I finished doing something in order to do something else, i. e. to work or to drink.
E. g. While walking down the sidewalk *(= Am. E.;* pavement = *Br. E.),* I stopped to chat with some friends. When I heard the sirens, I stopped chatting with my friends. I walked on . . .

*) Pushing is a participle, modifying Sisyphus, hence acting as a verbal adjective.

Gerunds = -ing forms
Exercise

Exercise 2:

Put the following words into the blanks in the sentences below:

to eat/eating

He remembered __________ canned mussels just before the cramps began.

He remembered __________ the canned mussels his friend had recommended.

to water/watering

He stopped __________ the horses because they had had enough to drink.

He stopped __________ the horses because they were thirsty.

to wash/washing

He had forgotten __________ the dishes and when his wife got home she was mad at him.

He had forgotten __________ the dishes and shifted his thoughts to happier things.

to paint/painting

She tried __________ as a way of forgetting her troubles.

She tried __________ the storm, the rain and clouds, but she did not succeed.

If we said a gerund signifies activity, the infinitive + to indicates intention or result, and often the participial form indicates the action has just ended.

Let's look at the last exercise question with to paint/painting again since it is perhaps a little tricky. ". . . painting as a way of forgetting" is an activity, a kind of therapy. She *intended* ". . . to paint the storm", and the speaker is concerned with the *result* of the activity, whether or not she performed well, whether the results were good or not.

Another set of words can take gerund or infinitive:

like, hate, love, start, begin.

The same rule applies as above, but, in all honesty, it is very difficult to show the difference between the two.

She liked to drink beer./She liked drinking beer.

It would very much depend on the context if a difference in meaning was intended.

They hate to leave parties early./
They hate leaving parties early.

It might be that the speaker is emphasizing the *"saying of goodbyes"* and thus would choose the latter form, the gerund, to show the act of leaving is hated. But there is, in this case, only a subtle difference, a nuance.

The Language of Money, Money

The mistake most frequently made in this category is confounding economIC and economICAL. The former is connected with trade or industry or a country's wealth, e. g.
The economic situation is presently not good.
Instability is a characteristic of the capitalist economic system.

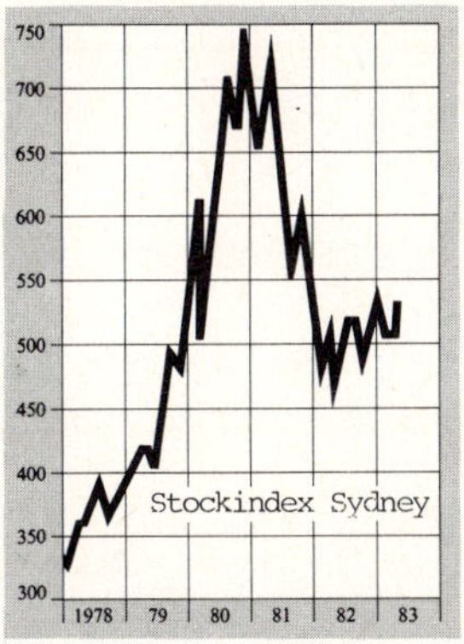

The latter means being efficient, not wasteful with money or things, e. g.,
It is economical to buy goods in quantity, i. e., the more you buy of a certain thing, the cheaper it will be.
It would be more economical if you didn't drive so fast,
i. e., you would save gasoline (= *Am. E.;* petrol = *Br. E.)*. Both words are adjectives and, unfortunately, their adverbial forms are the same: economically, a not very commonly seen form.
"We have an economic interest in the political stability of our trading partners". "Volkswagens are among the world's most economical cars, but not cheap to buy."
A verb quite similar to economical is *to economize,* which means to purposely cut down, to save, e. g.
We have to economize on energy use.
It's hard for a family to economize on food, but perhaps we might spend less on going out to dinner in expensive restaurants.
Notice the use of economize with the preposition ON, as well as: He *spent* all his allowance ON candy.
An *economist* is one who is trained in the science of *economics.* The major subject of this field of study is the *economy.* First, let's practise pronouncing these words: eCONomist [ɪˈkɒnəmɪst]; ecoNOMics [ˌiːkəˈnɒmɪks]; eCONomy [ɪˈkɒnəmɪ]. Say them a few times, OUT LOUD, until you can say them fluently.
Look back now and see if you can guess the German equivalents of the words just practised. Here they are upside down so you can check them:

economic = volkswirtschaftlich;
economical = sparsam, wirtschaftlich;
economize = sparen;
economist = Volkswirtschaftler;
economics = Volkswirtschaftslehre;
economy = Wirtschaft (the sober one is meant).

The Language of Money, Money

A similar confusion arises with the words SAVE and SPARE. Their meanings are not that far apart, but their usage is quite different. When I *save* money or anything else I am keeping it to use later. If I have a *spare* tire (= *Am. E.;* tyre = *Br. E.)* or *spare* bicycle or *spare* bedroom I have something ready to use whenever I need it. I don't know anyone who admits to having *"spare"* money, *spare* change perhaps, but we just don't say spare money.

Perhaps it would help if it was pointed out that you can put money *in* the bank, maybe *in* a savings account. I put most of my money in a checking account. Then I can pay bills or buy things by writing a check out for the amount. So, I put money *in* or sometimes we say *into* , an account at the bank. I rarely have very much money *in* my account, or I don't have much money in the bank, is another way of saying the same thing. I have an arrangement with my employer that the money I earn is automatically transferred into my bank account. (Es wird überwiesen. But this practice is not that common in the U.K. or in the U.S.A.) I can then take the money out of my account or *draw* it out.

Now you can check how well you have unterstood all this.

Exercise 1:

Fill in the appropriate word:

John Kenneth Galbraith is one of America's most famous 1__________ . He taught 2__________ at Harvard University. One of his important books about the U.S. 3__________ is called *The Affluent Society.*

Barclays Bank	26.20	470.–	478.–
B.A.T.Ind.	32.90	138.–	137.–
Beecham Group	11.40	341.–	336.–
Blue Circle Ind.	25	435.–	433.–
B.O.C. Int.	8.20	213.–	215.–
Boots P. Drug	12.10	269.–	270.–
Bowater „A"	16.40	230.–	232.–
Brit. Petrol.	28.90	390.–	398.–
Cadbury-Schw.	6.57	107.–	105.–
Coats Patons	5.71	65.50	66.–
Consol. Goldf.	35	569.–	567.–
Courtaulds	4.30	92.–	94.–
De La Rue	31.50	602.–	605.–
Distillers	16.80	214.–	220.–
Dunlop	5.71	64.–	64.–
Fisons	14.30	690.–	680.–
Gen. Electric.	3.64	212.–	212.–
Gr. Univ. St. „A"	18.60	520.–	523.–
Guest, K. & N.	11.40	161.–	161.–
Guinness, A.	7	108.–	108.–
Hawker Sidd.	13.30	302.–	308.–
Hoover „A"	0	125.–	120.–
ICI	27.10	518.–	524.–
Imp. Group	10.40	116.–	119.–
Lloyds Bank	30.50	540.–	541.–
Lonrho	12.90	98.–	97.–
Marks & Spenc.	6.57	193.–	197.–
Rank Org.	15.40	176.–	179.–
Shell Transp.	12.60	562.–	568.–
Thorn Emi	20.90	559.–	554.–
Turner & New.	4.30	56.–	56.–
Unilever	38.40	735.–	753.–
Vickers	16.70	105.–	106.–

Money, Money Exercises

Often, he has been rather critical about how the 4 __________ system of America affects the poor in that society. He writes in a clear style and is 5 __________ with words. He does not believe the Government should always 6 __________ on the money it gives out for the less advantaged. In his lifetime he has sold millions of his books. Certainly, he has been able to 7 __________ a lot of money from the profits. His critics have said that his 8 __________ policies can be compared to driving a car without having a 9 ______ tire. He has advocated that in the long run it would be more 10. __________ and also ethical to have a guaranteed minimum annual income for each American citizen. Is is difficult to measure the costs of such a policy, although many believe it would be socially ideal.

Exercise 2:

Now see if you know or can guess the following forms of payment: (use the words below)

A. The owner of an apartment house gets ______
B. A worker gets ______
C. An employee gets ______
D. An architect gets ______
E. A child gets ______
F. A government gets ______
G. A retired person gets ______
H. A waiter or waitress gets ______
I. A stockholder gets ______
J. An investor gets ______
K. A poor person (from public funds) gets ______
L. A poor person (from private funds) gets ______
M. An institution or firm gets ______
N. A soldier or sailor gets ______

1) a pension 2) an allowance 3) charity 4) wages 5) dividends 6) welfare 7) tips 8) taxes 9) rent 10) a salary 11) interest 12) a subsidy 13) a fee 14) pay.

Tenses
General Remark on Tenses

As you will all have experienced yourselves, the proper use of the tenses is not exactly easy. As usual we will concentrate on the most common mistakes by comparing the forms which are most frequently mixed up by students.

Perhaps you would like to test yourself? Translate the following sentences into English and pay attention to the choice of the tenses.

1. 1962 habe ich in New York Englisch studiert.
2. Damals habe ich noch bei meinen Eltern gewohnt.
3. Er studiert an der Londoner Universität Mathematik, aber zur Zeit arbeitet er in einer Fabrik, um Geld zu verdienen.
4. Er studiert schon seit drei Jahren.

Before you check the answers remember the following:

> The German use of tenses does not help you to find the right English tense to use!

Here are the solutions:

1. I studied English in New York in 1962.
2. At that time I was still living with my parents.
3. He studies mathematics at London University, but at the moment he is working in a factory to earn some money.
4. He has been studying for three years.

In order for you to decide which tense you have to choose, you should ask yourself the following questions:

1. What is my point of orientation (= the point of time from which I am looking at something) and what period of time am I speaking about, i.e. which tense do I have to choose?
2. Am I talking of an activity which is being carried on for some time, i.e. do I have to use the continuous form?

The following diagram and examples may help you to answer the above questions.

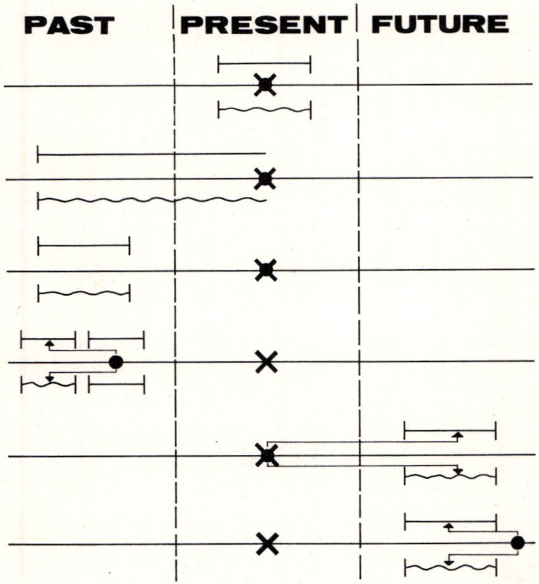

present	**simple**	I always *get up* at seven.
	cont.	I'*m learning* English at the moment
present	**simple perfect**	I'*ve had* a car for 2 years.
	cont.	I'*ve been* waiting since five o'clock.
past	**simple**	I *went* to school yesterday.
	cont.	I *was having* a bath when the telephone rang.
past perfect	**simple**	She *had* already *left* when he rang.
	cont.	I *had been waiting* for him for an hour when he came.
future	**simple**	I *will do* it tomorrow.
	cont.	I *will be dreaming* of you all night.
future perfect	**simple**	I *will have finished* the job by Friday.
	cont.	By the end of this year I *will have been living* here for ten years.

X = moment of speaking
● = point of orientation (Bezugspunkt)

Tenses
Present Simple and Continuous

Comparison of Simple Present and Present Continuous

We are almost certain that you must have heard and/or read the following rule quite a few times, but we'll say it again — just to make sure that you remember:

The present continuous is used for actions in progress which are incomplete or temporary.
Example: *I'm trying to explain this to you.*
The simple present is used for habitual, routine actions.
Example: *I always explain this to my students.*
It is also used for timeless statements which have nothing to do with the moment of speaking.
Example: *The sun rises in the east.*

Apart from the uses given above, both forms have other functions as well, which will be dealt with later.

Fortunately, there are some indicators which help you with your choice. Here is a short list of such "key words" and a few examples to demonstrate the use of the simple present and the present continuous respectively.

simple present	present continuous
always*)	now
never, rarely, seldom	at the moment
sometimes	at present
often	today
usually	this week
in general	this morning
as a rule, etc.	this year, etc.
I *always go* to work by tram,	but *this week* I'*m going* by car.
I *never wear* a hat,	but *today* I'*m wearing* one, because the sun is very hot.
I *usually eat* cake in the afternoon,	but *at the moment* I'*m slimming*, so I'm forbidden sweets.

---

*) All these adverbs may be used with other tenses as well, but when you use them together with a present tense, it's the simple present and not the continuous.

Present Simple and Continuous Exercises

Now let's do some exercises. Something simple first.

Exercise 1:
Put the verbs in their correct forms — present continuous or simple present.

1. *go*

   Susan: I ________________ now, Mum!

   Mum: Where ________________ , dear?

   Susan: I ________________ to my French course.

   Mum: Your French course?

   Susan: Yes, the holidays are over and I always ________________ to a French course on Mondays, remember?

   Mum: Oh, yes, of course. Bye-bye dear.

2. *wait*

   Bob: Hello, Jane. What are you doing here?

   Jane: Oh, I ________________ for Bill. I often ________________ for him after work.

3. *cook*

   Normally, I never ________________ in the evenings, but today I ________________ a special meal, because it's my husband's birthday.

Tenses
Present Simple and Continuous

4. *play*

Kay: What is that strange noise?

Frank: My neighbour ________________ the trumpet. He always ________________ it at this time of the day. He ________________ a lot, you know, but I can't hear any progress.

5. *speak*

We always ________________ German at home, but at the moment the whole family ________________ English, because we have a guest from the States.

6. *disturb*

Ann: I ________________ you?

Bob: No, you never ________________ me.

Exercise 2:

Put the verbs in brackets in their correct forms — present continuous or present simple. Look at each sentence carefully and ask yourself:

Does it express a general idea or is something mentioned which is done regularly? = simple present
or
Is it describing a momentary situation? = present continuous

1. The committee (meet) once a month to talk about current problems.
2. At the moment, the XX. International Toy Fair (take place) in Nuremberg.
3. The new government (try) to find a solution to the unemployment problem.
4. Every new goverment (try) to introduce a new political style.
5. In many European countries, the cost of living (rise) constantly.
6. When there is a rise in wages, prices automatically (rise) as well.
7. In our office we (change over) to automatic typewriters at the moment.
8. Water (boil) at 100 degrees centigrade.
9. The water (boil). You can make tea now.
10. At the XYZ factory they (introduce) a new form of worker co-determination (Mitbestimmung).

Were these exercises too easy for you? Here is one which is certainly more challenging.

Present Simple and Continuous Exercises

Exercise 3:

Here are some sentences which are taken from English and American newspapers. Change the following words into present simple or present continuous and put them into the sentences below.

burst, come, consider, depend, die off, fight, find, get, lie, lose, mean, offer, provide, spend, try, urge

1. Saudi Arabia, the world's largest oil exporter, ______________ its grip on the oil market now.
2. The governments of West Germany, France and Britain ______________ the Reagan administration to get back on speaking terms with the Soviet Union.
3. Along the border between Somalia and Ethiopia ______________ some of the least desirable territory in the world. But two rival armies ______________ bitterly over this parched (dürr) land at the moment.
4. When it ______________ to international trade, there's just no substitute for knowing the territory. Bank of America ______________ you experts in more countries than almost any other bank. That ______________ you ______________ first-hand knowledge of local markets. Your account officer ______________ you with information from around the world on new business opportunities.
5. Once every eighty to a hundred years the bamboo forests in China ______________ into flower and then ______________ . And that's bad news for the Giant Panda, which ______________ for its survival on huge amounts of bamboo.

Tenses
Present Simple and Continuous

6. After more than eight months of martial law (Kriegsrecht), many Poles ______________ day-to-day life increasingly difficult.
7. According to oil-industry experts, Saudi Arabia ______________ selling oil to certain companies.
8. El Salvador's political parties, from the far right to the moderate left, ______________ to settle their differences and hold the country together.
9. The Socialist party executives ______________ much of the summer preparing a programme for government.

Now let's turn to a different problem. We have said before that with words like *always,* etc., you use the simple present. There is however an exception to this rule. Look at the following example:

She is always eating cake!

This seems to be a blatant misuse of the continuous tense. The sentence is, however, correct. And this is the explanation:

> You use the present continuous with words like
> *always, forever, all the time, constantly, continually,* etc.
> for habitual actions if you want to express some sort of criticism, irritation or annoyance.

The sentence above could be followed by something like: *No wonder she is so fat!*

Now please express your irritation!

Exercise 4

A Make sentences and — if possible — say them aloud and give your voice an impatient ring!
Example: *He/always/borrow money from me.*
= He is always borrowing money from me!

1. He/always/borrow money from me.
2. She/forever/say no when you ask her to do you a favour.
3. He/constantly/complain about his bad health.
4. Those children/ask silly questions all the time.
5. My mother/continually/tell me that I am lazy.
6. He/constantly/change his mind.

General Remark on Continuous Forms

B Now say the sentences again and follow them up with a suitable remark from this list. Which remark fits which sentence?

a) They are really nerve-racking!
b) You just can't rely on what he says!
c) I'm really fed up with her silly remarks!
d) I don't think I can stand him much longer!
e) Don't you think that's unfair of her!
f) As if I were a millionnaire!

It's 1f, 2 ______________________

For the use of the present tense in conditional clauses → p. 143; as one of the possibilities of expressing future ideas → p. 118.

General Remark on the Use of the Continuous Forms

It is not always easy to decide whether to use a verb in its simple or in its continuous form. But one thing can be said in general:

> For a verb to be used in a continuous form, it must express some sort of activity which can be carried on uninterruptedly for some temporary period of time.

Take a sentence like
John is watching television at the moment.
The verb *watch* expresses an intentional (beabsichtigte) action which has a certain continuity. In the sentence
I can see John,
however, the verb *see* expresses an unintentional (unbeabsichtigte) action: As long as my eyes are open and my face is turned in John's direction, I can and will see him. To *see* is a faculty which you always have unless you have your eyes closed or are blind.

From what has been said so far we arrive at the conclusion that not all English verbs can have a continuous form. You wouldn't be able to say ✗ *I am seeing John* ✗ if you mean: *I can see him.* You could, however, say: *I am seeing John at five,* which means: *I have an appointment with John at five o'clock. See* is then no longer a verb of perception (Wahrnehmung), but means *to meet by appointment* or *to visit.*

Tenses
Verbs not Used in Continuous Form

Verbs Which are not Used in the Continuous Form

To help you with the decision (continuous or simple) it might be useful to ask yourself the following question:
Can I watch or observe somebody doing something?
If your answer is yes, you can put the verb in a continuous form. You could for example watch *John watching TV,* or *listening to the radio,* or *learning English,* or *working,* etc. But you could not possibly watch him *see or hear something,* or *have a car,* or *love Beethoven* and *hate rock music.* Those things are unwatchable, because they are states of affairs and not activities.

Now look at the following groups of verbs which do not normally form a continuous tense.

1. Verbs of perception

see, hear, smell, feel, taste.

These verbs are not used in a continuous form if they have their basic meaning, expressing an involuntary action. In that case they may be preceded by *can* without a major change in meaning.

Examples:
I *(can) see* John over there.
I *(can) hear* a strange noise.
I *(can) smell* snow in the air.
I *(can) feel* the wind in my face.
This soup *tastes* delicious.

If you want to express a voluntary action, you have to use the verbs *look* or *watch* for *see,* and *listen* for *hear.*

Examples:
I'*m looking* out of the window.
He *is watching* TV.
They *are listening* to a record.

The verbs *see, hear, smell, feel* and *taste* may, however, be uscd in the continuous, but then they have a different meaning.

Examples:
I *am seeing* John at five (treffen).
The judge *is hearing* the case tomorrow (anhören, verhandeln).
Why *are* you smelling the meat? (riechen an).
How *are* you *feeling* today? (sich fühlen).
I *am* just *tasting* the soup to see if there is enough salt in it (probieren).

Verbs not Used in Continuous Form

2. Verbs expressing emotions and wishes

like, love, adore, care, be fond of, be pleased, prefer;
dislike, hate, detest, loathe, mind, be angry, be annoyed;
fear, be afraid of;
want, wish, intend.

Want and *wish* can take a continuous form, but only in the present perfect! Example: I *have been wanting* a dog since I was a child.

3. Verbs of possession

belong to, have, own, possess; owe.

When *have* is used in expressions such as *"have a bath/shower/breakfast/tea,* etc." it can of course be used in the continuous.

4. Verbs expressing opinion or understanding

believe, think, feel, guess, suppose, mean, be of the opinion, feel certain, feel sure, know, expect;
understand, gather, see.

When *think* describes the process of mental activity, it can be used in the continuous form.

Examples:
What *are* you *thinking* about?
We *are thinking* of going to France for our next holiday.

Expect in the meaning of *"to wait for"* can also be used in the continuous form.

Examples:
She *is expecting* a baby.
Are you *expecting* anyone?

5. Other verbs

appear, seem; concern; consist; hold; matter; keep, etc.

Examples:
He *appears (seems)* to be very rich.
That *doesn't concern* me.
The novel *consists* of three main chapters.
It *doesn't matter* at all.
Don't keep asking me silly questions.

Exercise 5

Put the verbs in brackets in the correct form — simple or continuous. The verbs in italics have to be put in the past tense, the other verbs in the present.

1. A quiet evening at the Robinsons': Mr. Robinson (watch) TV, Mrs. Robinson (look through) a magazine, Susan (read) and Bob (listen) to his new record.

Tenses
Verbs not Used in Continuous Form

2. What you (think) of John's new car? – I (think) it's sheer madness to buy a car which uses as much petrol as that!
3. I (think) of you all the time.
4. The night was pitch-black. I *(not see or hear)* anything.
5. I (not see) a reason why I should stay any longer.
6. I can't put you through to Mr. Smith now. He (see) an important customer.
7. You (have) a car of your own at the moment?
8. You can't speak to Tom now, he (have) a shower.
9. I *(feel for)* my car keys when I suddenly remembered that they were in Mary's handbag.
10. I *(feel)* sure that I was right, but I didn't say anything.

Now let's do a final exercise with the simple present and the present continuous to see if you have grasped the main differences.

Bits & Pieces

Common Abbreviations

e.g., means *exempli gratia* in Latin (keep this esoteric knowledge to yourself – English-speaking people have long forgotten it) and in English: for example. ✗ f.ex. ✗ is not an abbreviation for anything! Always set, *e.g.*, off in commas. When you encounter, *e.g.*, while reading out loud, say: "for example" and <u>not</u> the letters 'EG'. Use *e.g.*, when you want to show several examples.

i.e., means *id est* in Latin and in English: that is; in other words; that means; that is to say. You can also say the letters 'IE' when reading aloud, unlike 'EG'. Use *i.e.* when you want to explain something, especially in a simpler fashion than you have just used. It should also be set off in commas, before and after.

etc. *etcetera* in Latin, meaning: a number of unspecified items. One can also read it out loud: and so forth, but ✗ a.s.f. ✗ does not exist as an abbreviation. Someone once said, when you see *etc.* it means the author has no more to say but wants to appear as if he did. Like the abbreviations above, etc., is always surrounded by commas.

Continuous or not? Exercises

Exercise 6

Choose the correct form and cross *a* or *b*.

1. Usually I a) go out / b) am going out on Saturday evenings,

   but today I a) stay / b) am staying at home.

2. Normally I a) like / b) am liking coffee better than tea,

   but at the moment I a) prefer / b) am preferring tea.

3. What a) do you think / b) are you thinking about?

4. What a) do you think / b) are you thinking of my new haircut?

5. He always a) goes / b) is going away at the weekend to see his parents.

6. You know, I'm really fed up with this situation.

   He a) always goes / b) is always going away at the weekend!

7. This bottle a) holds / b) is holding two litres.

8. I a) feel / b) am feeling much better than yesterday.

9. a) Don't you feel / b) Aren't you feeling that you should apologize to him?

10. I've always told you the truth and I a) don't lie / b) am not lying now.

a	b

Tenses
Present Perfect — 'for' and 'since'

Present Perfect with "for" and "since"

Unlike German, English uses the present perfect and not the simple present for actions which began in the past and are continuing into the present. This becomes particulary obvious when you have a German sentence like

Seit 1977 habe ich ein Auto.

which is translated into English by

I have had a car since 1977.

Look at the following illustration:

1977

I *had* a car in 1977.

NOW

I *have* a car now.

I *have had* a car since 1977.

As you use this form to express that something started in the past and is still true at the present moment, you use a present and a past form of the verb:

present: have past: had

The German preposition seit has two English equivalents:

for	since
two days	yesterday
the last week	last week
several months	December
some years	1972
a long time	I was at school

Present Perfect — 'for' and 'since' Exercises

From the above examples you'll see that *for* and *since* introduce different time phrases:

For is used for a period of time.
Since is used for a point of time.

Since hat einen Punkt auf dem i, es wird für den Zeit-*punkt* verwendet!

Exercise 7:
Put in *for* or *since*.

1. I haven't seen him __________ last week.
2. I have learnt English __________ eight years now, but I still make mistakes.
3. My mother has been with us __________ the last two weeks.
4. Germany has been a democracy __________ after the Second World War.
5. We haven't heard from him __________ ages (eine Ewigkeit).
6. He hasn't been at work __________ Easter.
7. I haven't eaten candy __________ I was a child.
8. __________ when have you known him?

Exercise 8
As most mistakes are due to German interference, we would like you to translate the following sentences into English.

1. Seit seinem Unfall ist er im Krankenhaus.
2. Ich warte schon seit einer Stunde auf dich! *(continuous)*
3. Seit seiner Scheidung ist er jeden Abend im Klub.
4. Ich habe seit einer Woche ein neues Auto.
5. Seit letztem Monat haben wir scheußliches Wetter.
6. Wir leben seit mehreren Jahren in München. *(continuous)*
7. Ich kenne ihn seit mehr als 10 Jahren, und er ist immer sehr zuverlässig gewesen.
8. Der Streik der Stahlarbeiter dauert nun schon vier Wochen.
9. Ich spiele seit zwei Jahren Tennis, aber es macht mir eigentlich keinen Spaß.
10. Sie wohnen seit Jahren in einem eigenen Haus.

Tenses
Present Perfect or Simple Past

Comparison of Present Perfect and Simple Past

Let's have a look at the diagram again:

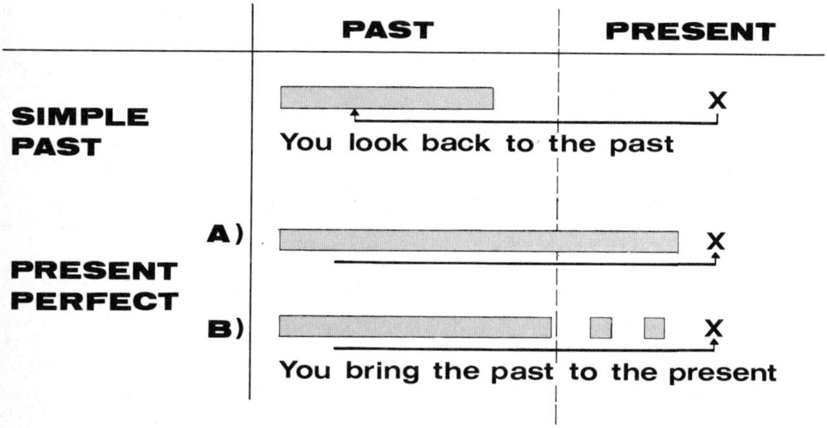

You can see from the diagram that you use the past tense for events which were completed in the past, whereas the present perfect has two functions. It indicates that A) something which started in the past continues into the present and B) the speaker refers to something which happened in the past and is significant for his present situation.

Now look at the following examples:

1. **I have had a car since 1977.**
What I say was true some time ago and is still true at the moment of speaking* =A

2. **A meeting has been arranged between the two opponents.**
I am talking about the present state of affairs without referring to the time something happened =B

3. **I've been to England (twice).**
What I am talking about has some effect on the present, is part of my present experience, although the action itself happened in the past. But when it happened is not relevant at the moment of speaking =B

The last point is certainly the most difficult one. So let's look at it in more detail:
Compare:
I have been to England.
and
I was there last week.

The difference in those two sentences is not in real time. Both sentences talk

* → Present perfect with *for* and *since*, p. 98

about the same event, your stay in England, which took place last week. But your orientation is different. In the first sentence you state a fact, talk about an experience, etc., and you are not in the least interested in the time it happened. Whereas in the second sentence you do emphasize the time the event happened, you mention the time *(last week),* and that is why you use the simple past tense.

All three examples could be followed by a sentence in the simple past stating a point of time in the past or providing other information which implies a reference to time, such as person, place, thing.

1. *I have had* a car since 1977. I *bought* it from a London car dealer. (The later mention of "car dealer" is a time indicator, e.g.: The dealer *was* located near Marble Arch.)
2. A meeting *has been arranged* between the two opponents. It *was arranged* by Mr. Smith, who acted as an intermediary.
3. I'*ve been* to England. I *was* there last week.

Although the question of when to use the simple past and when to use the present perfect is by no means an easy one, there are fortunately some indicators to help you with your choice. Here is a list of words with which to use the past or present perfect respectively:

past

yesterday
last week/month, etc.
a second/minute/week/year/
a million years, etc., ago
just now
in 1945/1972, etc.
in the Second World War
during the Russian Revolution
as a child
when I was at school
if you make statements
about dead people or
past events in history
or places you left, etc.

present perfect

ever
never
just
now
still
yet
already
recently
lately
of late
so far
until now
up to now
hitherto
since 1977
for ten years
all my life, etc.

Tenses
Present Perfect or Simple Past

Many of the adverbs given in the present perfect list may of course be used with other tenses as well, but when the choice is between present perfect and simple past, they are used with the present perfect.

A small problem arises with phrases like *this morning, this afternoon, this evening, this week,* etc., because you can use them with the past or the present perfect depending on whether the time mentioned is over or not. Look at the following examples:
John *has phoned* three times this morning.
____________ is said at 11 a.m. because the morning is not over yet.
John *phoned* three times this morning.
____________ is said at 3 p.m. for example, because the morning is over.

A very common mistake is made when people talking about date and place of birth. Mind the tense and say:
Where were you born?
I was born in Hamburg.
When were you born?
I was born in 1955.

Exercise 9
Let's start with something easy. If you look at the following sentences carefully enough, you will realize that each of them contains an indicator which will help you to put the verbs in brackets into the right tense. **Pay attention to the word order!**

1. I (begin) only recently to learn French.
2. You ever (see) Shakespeare's King Lear?
   No, I ________ , but I (see) the modern opera by Reiman some time ago.
3. She (be) very ill last month, but she (be) better lately.
4. Up to now we (be) lucky with the weather.
5. Frank (telephone) just now. He wants his car back.
6. You (have) three bottles of beer now, I think that's enough!
7. I just (finish) my job.
8. As a student I always (buy) my books second-hand.
9. You (have) lunch yet? – Yes, I (have) lunch at the canteen.
10. Doris Lessing (write) some very good stories.
11. Oscar Wilde (write) a number of very witty comedies.

It is a common mistake for German students to confuse the words *for* and *ago.* Would you like to test yourself and see if you get it right?

Fill in the gaps by using the following phrases:

a) *some minutes ago* b) *for two years*
c) *for some minutes* d) *two years ago*

Present Perfect or Simple Past Exercises

He was here ( ), but he went out ( ). He lived in Paris ( ), but now he has lived here ( ).

Solution: (c), (a), (d), (b)

Ago is always used with the simple past tense, whereas *for* is used with the past if it means (zwei Jahre etc.) lang and with the present perfect if it means seit (zwei Jahren etc.). Look at the following examples:

I went to France 10 years ago. = vor 10 Jahren
I lived there for 8 years. = 8 Jahre lang
I have been back for 2 years. = seit 2 Jahren

Exercise 10

Fill in the gaps by using the phrases below the sentences.

1. My first car was a Ford Capri. I bought it second hand ________________ and I had it ________________ . When it broke down, I bought a Mercedes which I've had ________________ .

   a) *ten years ago* b) *for some years* c) *for the last four years*

2. I have lived here ________________ . Only once, ________________ , I thought I should see something of the world and went to Australia. But I was so homesick that I didn't stay ________________ .

   a) *about 20 years ago* b) *for almost all my life* c) *for more than two months.*

3. ________________ a strange species of animals called dinosaurs lived on earth They were here ________________ and have been extinct (ausgestorben) ________________ .

   a) *for millions of years* b) *for a comparatively short period* c) *about 170 million years ago*

4. We decided to go to France for our next holiday. Well, I learnt French at school ________________ . But that was ________________ and I've never spoken a word of French since. So I took a course at night school where I've been studying that tongue-twisting language ________________ .

   a) *for some months now* b) *25 years ago* c) *for four years*

5. You play the piano, don't you? — Well, I used to play it ______________ . I had lessons ______________ . But I don't think I can play anymore. I haven't touched a key ______________ .

   a) *for four or five years* b) *for ages* c) *a long time ago*

6. I'm sorry, Mr. Brown isn't in his office. He went out ______________ . He waited for your phone call ______________ . — You didn't get through? But our line's been free ______________ .

   a) *a moment ago* b) *for more than an hour* c) *for the last two hours*

As you know now, the present perfect tense is concerned with the present state of affairs whereas the past is used to tell what happened, how it happened, why it happened, etc. Thus many newspaper articles start with a sentence in the present perfect to describe the situation and go on with a more detailed report of the events in the past. Look at the following example:

"A 9th century Koran manuscript *has been stolen* from an antique shop in Portobello Road. The thieves, who *broke* into the shop some time Saturday night, *came in* through a back window. They *didn't take* anything else but the manuscript which was worth about £40,000."

Exercise 11
Here are a few newspaper clippings. They all have opening sentences in the present perfect. We want you to write one or two more sentences in the past to continue the story and fill in a few details. But first of all look at the clippings:

①
OIL IN S. YEMEN
An Italian company *has found* oil in commercial quantities in Marxist governed South Yemen.

② **Sir Derek Rayner**, the Government's special adviser on how to cut costs, *has been called in* to scrutinise*) the Health Service's £12,000 million-a-year spending programme.

*) genau untersuchen

Present Perfect or Simple Past Exercise

③
A sit-in by 54 homeless blacks in the sanctuary of St George's Anglican Cathedral in Cape Town *has been broken* after 23 days during which they have refused practically all food and nourishment.

④
BANKING PAY RISE
By Our Industrial Staff
Members of the Banking, Insurance and Finance Union *have voted* to accept an 8 1/2 per cent pay offer made by the "Big Five" clearing banks.

⑤
10m TINS OF U.S. SALMON* HELD
More than ten million 1/2 lb cans of imported American salmon *have been held back* from distribution in Britain or returned by the public following a government warning in February that they may be contaminated**) by botulism.

*) Lachs **) verdorben

⑥
ANGLO-FRENCH ATOM PROTEST TO GREECE
By Our Athens Correspondent
Britain and France *have protested* against a call by Mr Papandreou Greece's Socialist Prime Minister, for their independent nuclear forces to be included in any future East-West nuclear disarmament negotiations.*)

*) Abrüstungsverhandlungen

⑦
By Our Melbourne Correspondent
Aboriginal militants *have threatened* to disrupt the Brisbane Commonwealth Games in September.

Now use the following cues to make sentences. The verbs in italics have to be put in the passive voice!

Example:

1. Oil/*discover*/near capital of Aden
   The oil was discovered near the capital of Aden.

2. He/*appoint*/yesterday/after a heated discussion in Parliament.
3. Police/step in/force/them to leave the sanctuary. Leaders/*arrest.* Others/*take*/to hospital.
4. Decision/*announce*/yesterday after tough negotiations.
5. When accident/become known/inquiry/*start.* Cans/*return* and *destroy.*
6. Mr. Papandreou/make call/at Athens last week.
7. They/*involve*/in a long-term Soviet-inspired plot.

Tenses
Present Perfect or Simple Past

Exercise 12
Now let's have a general revision on the past and present perfect.
Put the verbs in brackets in the correct tenses. Read each sentence carefully,

look for indicator words, find out if a state of affairs is expressed or an action in the past and then make your choice. Mind the word order! Verbs in italics require the passive voice.

1. Wage negotiations for West Germany's 2,600,000 public workers *(put)* to mediation (Schiedsverfahren) yesterday after breaking down.
2. So far the Interior Ministry (negotiate) with the trade unions, without success though.
3. Sheikh Yamani, oil minister of Saudi Arabia, (be) in London this week. He (arrive) on Monday and (start) his talks with British politicians immediately after his arrival.
4. One hundred police officers (join) the hunt for the killer of 11-year-old Susan Maxwell, whose body *(find)* on Thursday.
5. Sixteen people (die) so far this month. They were victims of a drug war which (break out) between rival gangs of drug dealers some weeks ago.
6. More than £1m worth of cocaine *(seize* = beschlagnahmen) by FBI agents. This *(announce)* by an official speaker yesterday.

Exercise 13
Same instructions as above.

1. A: Look what I (buy) myself today. Isn't it a beautiful dress!
   B: Yes, it suits you very well. Where you (buy) it? How much it (cost)?
2. A: You ever (hear) of a poet named Burns?
   B: Yes, he (live) some two hundred years ago. He (be) Scottish, I think.
3. A: Imagine, I (lose) my car keys!
   B: Oh God, do you know where you (lose) them?

Present Simple and Continuous Exercise

The next day:

B: You (find) your car keys?

A: Yes, I hadn't lost them after all, they (be) at the bottom of my shopping bag.

4. A: Do you know that John (write) a play?

B: Yes of course, he (write) it when he (be) in Greece with us.

5. A: How long you (live) here?

B: I (live) here for three years. But before I (come) here, I (live) in Burma for six years.

Comparison of Present Perfect Simple and Continuous

We have already dealt with the present perfect, especially with its relationship to the simple past tense, but we haven't looked at its continuous form so far. Very often the continuous form is just used to emphasize the duration of an activity without any major changes in meaning, as can be seen in the following examples:

Bits & Pieces

Pronunciation Tip: polysyllabic words ending with:

-ate	-ally
-able	-ably
-ible	-age

never have their stress on the suffix (= last syllable[s]). Very often the suffix is underemphasized, making it difficult to hear and, thus, often misspelled. Look in a dictionary where the main accent falls on these words:
credible; practically; suitable; predicate; comfortable; probably; indiscriminate; heritage; discourage; finally;
The final vowel is always short, i. e., ə or ĭ as in *about* or *ship*.

present perfect simple	present perfect continuous
I *have lived* here for three years.	I *have been living* here since 1979.
He *has studied* English for five years.	He *has been studying* English for five years.
I *have waited* for more than three hours.	I *have been waiting* for more than three hours.

Tenses
Present Perfect Simple and Cont.

This is particularly true for verbs which in themselves express a certain continuity or duration, such as *live, learn, study, wait, work,* etc.

There is, however, a difference in usage depending on whether you want to tell someone what you have been occupied with *(present perfect continuous)* or whether you want to talk about the result or state a fact *(present perfect simple).*

present perfect simple	present perfect continuous
I *have written* six letters since breakfast. *(You give the result in the form of an exact number)*	I *have been writing* letters since break-fast. *(You talk about your activity)*
I *have typed* that letter of yours. *(The letter is finished)*	I *have been typing* that letter of yours. *(And I still haven't finished)*
He *has eaten* my chocolates. *(All of them, nothing is left)*	He *has been eating* my chocolates. *(I could stop him, some of them are left)*

So we can say that you use the present perfect simple for completed actions (if the time of completion is irrelevant) and the present perfect continuous for uncompleted actions.

Exercise 14

Look at the following pairs of sentences and try to explain why the present perfect simple and the present perfect continuous are used respectively.

1. a) I have travelled a lot in my life.
   b) I have been travelling a lot these last few years.
2. a) I have cleaned the flat.
   b) I have been cleaning the flat all morning.
3. a) I have already checked the figures on your tax return (Steuererklärung).
   b) I have been checking the figures on your tax return.

Simple Past and Past Continuous

Exercise 15

Put the verbs in brackets into their correct forms (present perfect simple or continuous). Sometimes both forms are possible.

1. I (look through) my wardrobe and (sort out) a few old clothes. I shall throw them away, or do you know anyone who can use them?
2. I (look through) my books for the one you wanted, but I (not find) it yet.
3. You (finish) the job? — No, I (work) at it for the last two hours, but I (not finish) yet.
4. I (try) to teach you some manners all my life, but I don't seem to have been very successful.
5. We (live) here for six months and we like it very much.
6. He (work) since seven o'clock this morning.

Comparison of Simple Past and Past Continuous

The past continuous is used for past actions whose limits are neither known nor relevant. What we are interested in when we use this tense is the action, not the result or the completion of an action.

The simple past*) is used if you want to tell a story in the past, if you want to relate past events. Compare the following sentences:

simple past	past continuous
At seven it *was* already quite dark. *(A fact is stated)*	It *was getting* darker and darker. *(A progression is described)*
What *did* you *do* yesterday evening? — I *wrote* three letters. *(Completed action, result)*	What *were* you *doing* yesterday evening? — I *was writing* letters. *(Description of an action in progress; result is not important)*
I *had* lunch at twelve. *(I started at twelve)*	At twelve, I *was having* lunch. *(I started before twelve and was in the middle of my lunch)*
He always *rang* me at 11 p.m. *(I didn't mind)*	He *was* always *ringing* me at 11 p.m. *(I was annoyed)* **)

*) For the use of the simple past in conditional clauses → "Conditional-clauses", p. 143

**) For the use of the continuous tense with words like *always*, → Comparison of simple present and present continuous, p. 88

Tenses
Simple Past and Past Continuous

Now look at the pictures and the sentences which go with them.

I was having a bath

while

my wife was getting dressed

Two actions in the past which happened at the same time and were continued for a while.

I was having a bath

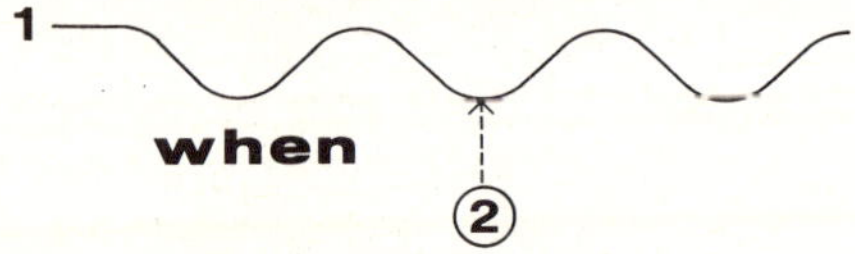

when

the telephone rang

One action was in progress (having a bath) when a second action set in.

I got out of the bath tub

and

answered the phone

Two actions follow each other: first I got out of the bath tub, then I went to the phone.

Simple Past and Past Continuous Exercices

Exercise 16

Put the verbs in brackets into the simple past or the past continuous.

1. Tom (talk) on the phone when I (arrive). When he (see) me, he (put down) the receiver.
2. When he (leave) his office he (put on) his coat because it (rain).
3. When he (leave) his office, he (wear) a coat.
4. I (get up) at six, (have) breakfast, (take) a shower and (go out) just in time to catch my train.
5. I (get up) when the postman (ring). (2 possibilities)
6. I normally (go) to lunch at noon.
7. It (be) quite cold last night.
8. When it (get) lighter we (know) that we (approach) the end of the tunnel.
9. What you (do) at the weekend? Well, I (read) a lot. You (finish) the book you (tell) me about the other day?

Exercise 17

The use of the simple and continuous forms of the past becomes particularly apparent in a continuous narration. Here are two passages of English literature. Put the verbs in brackets into the correct past tense.

Ⓐ

"On the fourteenth of July the Forestiers (go over) to a gala dinner at Monte Carlo, and they (give) their staff leave to go to Cannes. It (be) the national holiday, and in Cannes they (dance) in the open air under the plane trees, there (be) fireworks, and from far and near the people (come in) to have a good time. The Hardys had sent their servants out too, but they (sit) at home, and their two little boys (be) in bed. Fred (play) patience and Lady Hardy (work) at a piece of tapestry to cover a chair. Suddenly there (be) a ring of the bell and a loud knocking on the door."

(Somerset Maugham, The Lion's Skin)

Ⓑ

"I (feel) I (fall) asleep and then all at once something (catch) my attention. My eyes were focussed on a spot on the edge of the chaparral (Dornengestrüpp), but I not (look), or (think), or (talk) to myself. My feelings (be) clear bodily sensations; they not (need) words. I (feel) I (rush) through something indefinite. I (feel) the rush in my stomach. Something (pull) me into the chaparral. I (can) distinguish the dark mass of the bushes in front of me. I (can) see every individual bush as if I (look) at them in a dark twilight."

(Carlos Castaneda, Tales of Power)

Tenses
Simple Past and Past Perfect

Comparison of Simple Past and Past Perfect *)

Would you like to test yourself again? One of the verbs in the following sentences has to be put in the past perfect tense, the other one in the simple past tense. Have a go at it! Mind the position of the adverbs.

1. When I (come) home, she already (prepare) supper.
2. He (live) in Port Elizabeth for eight years, when I (visit) him for the first time.
3. They only met at long intervals. They (see) each other in London in 1972, and they last (meet) ten years before in the Far East.

Solution:
1. came, had prepared 2. had lived, visited 3. saw, had met

Perhaps it is useful to have a look at the diagram again in order to understand the rule.

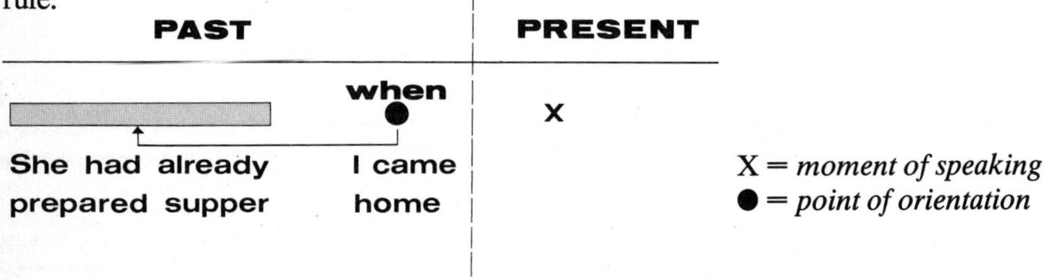

You are talking about something which happened in the past:

When I *came* home.

This is your point of orientation. Then you want to express something which had happened even before that point:

she *had* already *prepared* supper.

*) Past perfect in conditional clauses → Conditional Clauses, p. 143

Simple Past and Past Perfect Exercices

And that is when you use the past perfect tense. It is the past of the past, so to speak.

There are again some indicators for the use of the past perfect:
already, just, yet, still, since, for, etc.

Here are a few examples:
He *had just left* when I arrived. They *had lived/been living* in Berlin *for five years* when the war broke out. She *had still not finished* school when her parents divorced.

Sometimes, however, you could use the simple past tense instead of a past perfect without much difference in meaning, e.g.:

We went home as soon as the lesson *ended/had ended.*

But be careful, there may be confusion if you use the wrong tense. Look at the following two sentences:

1. When I arrived at the party everyone *went* home.

2. When I arrived at the party everyone *had gone* home.

In sentence 1 my appearance at the party caused people to go home, whereas in sentence 2 I was obviously much too late and nobody was there any longer.

If you talk about past events and use words like *after, before, first, then, later,* etc., you use the simple past tense since the temporal relationship between the events is then made clear by the adverbs, e.g.:
The children had an exciting day. *First* they *went* to Birmingham by train. *Then* they *visited* a coal mine. *Later* in the day they *were taken* to the pictures and *after the cinema* they *had* a lovely meal at . . .

Exercise 18

Put the verbs in brackets in their correct tenses — simple past or past perfect. Mind the word order!

1. Israel's last bombing of Beirut (outrage) President Reagan. It was unnecessary, because the PLO (make) already its last concession.
2. Financial experts (anticipate) the crisis for months, but for the man in the street it (come) as a surprise.
3. When President Gemayel (be killed) he (be) in office for a very short time only.
4. For months France (be battered) by terrorist attacks when last week the climax (be reached) with the anti-Semitic shooting spree at Goldenberg's restaurant that (leave) six people dead.
5. I knew that I always (react) aggressively, but I couldn't help it.
6. I knew that I (react) aggressively, and I apologized later.

Tenses
Future

The Future Tenses

You will certainly know that there are several possibilities in English to express a future idea. Here is a short survey of the different forms and functions before we deal with them individually:

FUNCTION / FORM	intention	prediction	definite future arrangements/planned activities	description of future activity or event
will/shall + infinitive	I'll help you. I'll wash my car. tomorrow.	Tomorrow will be cloudy with sunny intervals.		
will/shall + continuous				I'll be washing my car tomorrow morning. I'll be seeing him tomorrow.
going to	I'm going to talk to him about this problem.	Look at those clouds! It's going to rain soon.	I'm going to spend my next holiday in England. What are you going to do this evening?	
present continuous			What are you doing this evening? I'm going to the theatre.	
simple present			The new term starts on September 21.	

1. will/shall + infinitive

Before we go into the problems of usage, there is one word to be said about the form of this tense. In speaking you normally use the short form, which is *'ll* for *will* and *shall*. *Shall* has only future meaning with the first person singular or plural,

Future: will/shall + infinitive/+ continuous

i.e. you can say *I/We shall do that,* but not *You shall do that,* because in the latter sentence *shall* has a modal meaning which expresses the idea of sollen.

will/shall + infinitive is normally used
- for predictions: *It'll rain tomorrow.*
- for decisions taken at the moment of speaking:
  A: *"That's too heavy for me!"*
  B: *"Come here, I'll help you."*
- in if-clauses (→ p. 143):
  If you aren't careful, you'll hurt yourself.

There are some verbs and phrases which are often followed by this form:
think, hope, know, suppose, be sure, believe, well, all right, o. k., etc.
Here are some examples with these verbs:

I hope he will join us. I don't think they will give in. I suppose we'll have to do that ourselves. I'm sure he won't give us away (verraten). A: "You shouldn't go there." — B: "O. k., I won't.

Don't confuse the following:

I will	=	ich werde
ich will	=	I want to

2. will/shall + continuous

This form is used to describe a future activity or event. It is <u>not</u> used to express intention!

Compare the following dialogues:

A: That car of yours is rather dirty, isn't it?
B: Oh, shut up. I know it is. <u>I'll wash it</u> → decision taken at the
tomorrow morning. moment of speaking

A: Can I call you tomorrow morning?
B: No, not in the morning. <u>I'll be washing</u> → description of
my car then. Ring some time in the afternoon. future activity

As you will see from the above examples, the two forms are not interchangeable. Perhaps you would like to try and explain the difference between the following two sentences yourself?

a) I'll see him tomorrow.
b) I'll be seeing him tomorrow.

If you want to check your explanation, look up the key.

Tenses
Future

German students often think that the form *will be doing* is rarely used in English and that they can do without it. But this is not so. What's an informal way of saying good-bye, for example? — *See you later!* or: I'll be seeing you!

Exercise 19
Let's put the above rules into practice. Insert the correct future tense — will/shall + infinitive or + continuous of the verbs in brackets.

1. A: "What are your plans for the weekend?"
   B: "I ______________________ my parents-in-law." (go and see)
2. A: "I wanted to ask John to come round and see me some time next week."
   B: I ______________________ him tomorrow evening. Shall I ask him?" (see)
3. *(At a restaurant)*
   A: "May I take your order, Sir?"
   B: "Yes, I ______________________ a steak and a salad, please." (have)
4. A: "Would you like another cup of coffee, John?"
   B: "No, thank you. I think I ______________________ along." (run)
5. Tomorrow at this time we ______________________ over the Gulf of Arabia, if all goes well. (fly)
6. I promise that I ______________________ late this time. (not be)
7. Open a deposit account (Sparkonto) with us and your money ______________________ immediately ______________________ earning at a good rate of interest. (commence = anfangen, beginnen)

Future: going to Exercise

3. going-to

This form, which is probably the most widely used future tense of all, is typical for informal style. It is used for
- — intentions: *I'm going to talk to him about that.*
- — planned activities or definite future arrangements: *I'm going to spend my next holiday in England.*
- — predictions often made on the basis of observations made at the moment of speaking or of first-hand knowledge: *Look at these clouds. It's going to rain soon.*

Very often this form is used with an adverb indicating near future, but it is not restricted to the near future at all. It sometimes occurs in if-clauses, but the normal tense for them is will/shall + infinitive.

If you compare what has been said about will/shall + infinitive with the above remarks on the going-to-future, you will realize that both forms can be used for intentions and predictions. Here are some examples to illustrate the difference:

1. *I'll do* that for you.	:	I promise you now.
I'm going to do that for you	:	because I promised you some time ago.
2. *You'll have* an accident one day!	:	You are a very bad driver.
You're going to have an accident!	:	You are driving very badly at the moment.
3. I'm sure *he will come.*	:	if you ask him.
He's going to come.	:	I know because he told me.

Predictions made with the going-to form are normally based on immediate, first-hand knowledge or experience whereas predictions with will/shall + infinitive are much more general.

Tenses
Future

Exercise 20
Put the verbs in brackets in their correct future tense — will/shall + infinitive or going-to.

1. Unless we start to think about solutions now, there (be) tremendous energy problems in twenty years' time.
2. Watch out! The branch (break)!
3. He has never studied seriously. I'm sure he (fail) his exam.
4. A student who never studies seriously (fail) the exam.
5. Mr. A. (try) presumably to advance his own men into the vacancies in the politbureau.
6. Have you heard that Jane (have) a baby?
7. A: "Oh bother! I've made a typing error again!"
   B: "Come here! I (type) that letter for you."
8. A: "What are you doing this evening?"
   B: "I (write) letters."

4. present continuous

This form, like the going-to form, is used for definite future arrangements or planned activities:
What are you doing this evening? — I'm going out.

The two forms are often interchangeable, but not always, as you will see below. To avoid confusion with the present tense, this form should always be used with a time adverb pointing into the future. Of course it cannot be used with verbs which do not take a continuous form (→ p. 94 ff.).

As we have said above, this form is used for planned activities. So it seems only logical that it is restricted to verbs which can express such planned activities. *I am leaving soon* is o. k., because you can plan your leaving. ✗ *It is raining soon* ✗ is wrong, because you cannot possibly arrange for it to rain. You have to say: *It is going to rain/will rain soon.*

5. simple present

This form is the least frequently used of all. Its usage is restricted to
- statements about timetables and the like:
  The plane leaves at 5.45 p. m. Tomorrow is Monday.
- definite future arrangements for which alteration seems impossible and which are not necessarily made by the speaker himself:
  The written part of the examination begins at 9.30.

Future: present continuous/ simple present Exercises

Perhaps this clue can help you with your choice: If you can add *due to,* you can use the simple present: The plane *is due to leave* at 5.45 = The plane *leaves* at 5.45.

Exercise 21

Put the verbs in brackets in their correct future tense — going-to, present continuous or simple present.

1. New Year's Eve (fall) on a Monday this year.
2. The new theatre (be opened) next week.
3. I can't come round tomorrow. I (go) to the doctor's.
4. The newspapers say that prices (rise) again.
5. I (fly) to Paris next Monday.
6. The last train to Ipswich (leave) at 11.16. p.m.

Now let's have a final exercise on the future tenses.

Exercise 22

Translate the following sentences into English and use the appropriate future form.

1. Wir brauchen bald ein neues Auto. Unser altes fällt schon fast auseinander.
2. Wir werden uns dieses Mal einen Mercedes kaufen.
3. Ich habe gehört, daß Sie auswandern wollen. Sie werden sich am Anfang wahrscheinlich ziemlich einsam fühlen.
4. Morgen fliege ich für sechs Wochen nach Australien. Es wird eine lange Reise, aber man zeigt während des Flugs Filme, um die Zeit zu vertreiben.
5. Weihnachten fällt dieses Jahr auf einen Sonntag.
6. Ich hoffe, daß er zu unserer Party kommt.
7. Er wird eines Tages im Zuchthaus enden!
8. Morgen um diese Zeit werde ich schon am Strand liegen.
9. Ich werde meinen nächsten Urlaub in den Bergen verbringen.
10. Der Kurs beginnt am 15. Mai und dauert bis zum 4. Juni.

Adverbs
Formation of Adverbs

Formation of Adverbs

There are three different types of adverbs:

1. original adverbs:	here, now, yet, today, even, quite, early, always, very, also, doubtless, etc.
2. derived adverbs:	slowly, fully, truly, immediately, possibly, happily, shyly, basically, publicly
3. adverbial phrases:	in a friendly way/manner/fashion (used for adjectives ending in -ly)

The adverb of good is well

Normally, students at your level have no difficulties with spelling rules any more. But perhaps you would like to do the following exercises to check whether you've got any problems. If you have, we must refer you to your grammar book. But don't do the exercises only for spelling's sake! Pay attention to the function the adverb has in the sentence and to its position.

Exercise 1

Complete the sentences by using the adverb forms of the adjcctives given in brackets.

1. He searched the room ________________ . (systematic)
2. I ________________ understand that you refused his offer. (full)
3. The flat was ________________ furnished with everything you needed. (comfortable)
4. How do you sign your business letters? — I always use "Yours ________________ " (true)
5. It was ________________ announced that there would be a cut-off of electricity for one hour. (public)
6. They came in ________________ . (noisy)
7. If you want to attack me, do it ________________ (open), not ________________ . (cowardly)

8. She smiled ________________ at me not knowing if she could trust me. (shy)

9. He did everything he had to do ________________ (quick) and ________________ . (good)

Exercise 2

Rephrase the sentences by finding an adverb for the noun phrase:

Example: He completed this task *with success.* =
He completed this task successfully.

1. He sat there *in silence.*
2. She watched me *with curiosity.*
3. The cat jumped down from the table *with grace.*
4. He left the room *in fury.*
5. They answered all my questions *with patience.*
6. He greeted me *with enthusiasm.*
7. When he addressed me again, he spoke *with complete indifference.*
8. *From a political point of view,* this decision was unwise.
9. *In legal terms,* what he has done is a crime.

Exercise 3

Rephrase the sentences in the following way, using an adverb:

Example: He did everything for her *because of his deep love.* =
He did everything for her *because he loved her deeply.*

1. He has a legible (leserlich) handwriting. He writes . . .
2. There is a yearly issue of our report. We . . .
3. She gave me a friendly smile.
4. His was an early marriage.
5. When I said this, she gave me a reproachful (vorwurfsvoll) look.
6. He made an angry reply.
7. She heaved a deep sigh.
8. You have done some very good work.

Adverbs
Comparison of Adverbs

❗ The adverbs *far, long* and *much* can only be used in questions or negative sentences. In positive sentences they are replaced by *a long way, a long time* and *a lot of.*
Although a sentence like ✗ I have much money ✗ seems grammatically all right, English speaking people just wouldn't say it. They say: *"I have a lot of money"*, instead.

Exercise 4
Put in *far, long, much* or *a long way, a long time, a lot of.*

1. I don't like her ________________ .
2. He's got ________________ time.
3. It is still quite ________________ to London.
4. My grandmother can't walk very ________________ .
5. Could you wait a moment? I won't be ________________ .
6. We had to wait ________________ .

Comparison of Adverbs

In general, we can say that the same rules apply as for the comparison of adjectives, (→ p. 50) i. e.:

One-syllable adverbs, such as *fast, hard, soon, late, near,* etc., and the two-syllable adverb *early* form their comparison by adding *-er, -est.*
fast — fast**er** — fast**est**
hard — hard**er** — hard**est**

Adverbs ending in *-ly* form their comparison with *more* and *most*:
carefully — more carefully — most carefully
sensibly — more sensibly — most sensibly

There are however a few exceptions to this rule:

well	better	best
badly / ill	worse	worst
little	less	least
much	more	most
far	farther / further	farthest*) / furthest*)

*) For the use of farther/further → Adjectives, p. 51

Comparison/Use of Adverbs Exercises

Constructions with Comparisons

The constructions with comparisons are exactly the same as with adjectives. So we will just give you the three main constructions again and would like to refer you back to page 54 ff. if you need more detailed information.

They worked as fast as they could.
He worked faster than you did.
He worked fastest of all.

Exercise 5
Complete the sentences by putting the adverbs in brackets in their right form.

1. I tried to call you ________________ this week, but you weren't in. (early)
2. He was certainly treated ________________ than you were. (badly)
3. He behaved ________________ than the rest of you! (sensibly)
4. He was ________________ known of all and still won a prize! (little)
5. I don't know, I seem to work much ________________ than anyone else and still earn ________________ . (hard/little)
6. They all performed very well, but Jane played ________________ . (well)
7. He played ________________ than ever. (well)
8. The ________________ you go, the ________________ you have to watch the road. (fast/carefully)
9. He tried to speak to me as ________________ as possible, but you could see that he had to try very hard. (politely)

Use of Adverbs

So far we have dealt with the formation and the comparison of adverbs; now we'll have a look at the way adverbs are used. To deal adequately with this problem, we have to include the use of the adjective as well, because it is by comparing the two that the use of the adverb becomes particularly obvious.

Look at the following sentences:

1. *He* is **stupid.**
2. He is a **stupid** *man.*
3. He made a **stupid** *mistake.*

Adverbs
Use of Adverbs

In the three sentences above, *stupid* is an adjective which refers to the subject *He* in sentence 1, and to the nouns *man* and *mistake* in sentences 2 and 3. If you wanted to get sentence 1—3 as answers, you would have to ask the following questions:

1. What is he like?
   He is stupid.
2. What sort of man is he?
   He is a stupid man.
3. What sort of mistake did he make?
   He made a stupid mistake.

There are many more examples of the use of adjectives as modifiers (nähere Bestimmungen) to nouns and pronouns in the preceding chapter on adjectives (p. 50—60).

Now compare this sentence:

4. He *reacted* stupidly.

As you know, *stupidly* is an adverb. The word *ad·verb* itself says that it belongs somehow to the verb, that it modifies the verb. In this case none of the above questions would be appropriate to elicit sentence 4 as an answer. You would have to ask:

4. In which way did he react?
   He reacted stupidly.

But adverbs also modify other words than verbs. As you will see from the following examples, they modify adjectives (5), other adverbs (6) and even whole sentences (7).

5. *He* is extremely *stupid.*
6. He *reacted* extremely *stupidly.*
7. Stupidly, *he made a mistake.*

In German the translation for *stupid/stupidly* in sentences 1—6 would be dumm. Only in sentence 7 would the German word show that it is an adverb and say dummerweise. In other words, German won't tell you if you have to use an adverb or an adjective. You have to ask yourself: "Which word does it refer to?" and then make up your mind. If it refers to a noun or pronoun, use an adjective — otherwise you use an adverb. This is not always easy to decide.
Compare the following sentences:

8. *He* looks stupid.
9. He *looked* stupidly *at* me.

Although both sentences have the verb *look,* in sentence 8 *look* means aussehen and so *stupid* refers to *he* (*looks* could be replaced by *is*), whereas in sentence 9 the verb is *to look at* = anschauen and it is modified by the adverb

Use of Adverbs Exercise

stupidly (*looked* could not be replaced by *was!*). Here are a few more examples:

10. I *consider* him *clever.*
11. I *carefully considered* his suggestion.
12. The soup *tastes good.*
13. I *cautiously tasted* the hot soup.

Sentences 10 and 12 could again be changed into *He is clever* and *The soup is good.* This is not possible in sentences 11 and 13.

Now we think it's high time for another excercise, don't you? Here you are.

Exercise 6

Fill the gaps with the words in brackets (in the order given) and put them in their correct forms — adjective or adverb.

1. From an ________________ point of view, this problem seems ________________ difficult to solve. (economic/extreme)
2. ________________ speaking, these measures are inevitable. (economic)
3. Some people consider him ________________ , others regard him as only ________________ . (intelligent/clever)
4. Prices are rising at an ________________ rate. (incredible) They are ________________ high. (tremendous)
5. It is ________________ that he missed the train, but it is not very ________________ (conceivable = vorstellbar/likely)
6. A general election might ________________ produce a result in which no party has an absolute majority. (conceivable)
7. The cake smelt ________________ and tasted ________________ . (wonderful/ delicious)
8. The story he told us is ________________ . (unbelievable)
9. He was ________________ tall. (unbelievable)
10. A ________________ wise decision is not ________________ a ________________ one. (political/necessary/popular)

Adverbs
Use of Adverbs

Exercise 7

Would you like to do a test — not only on adverbs, but on your personality? Then complete the following questions with the right words from the list below. You are given the words in their adjectival form and you have to decide yourself whether you need an adverb or an adjective. The hidden word puzzle below may help you with your decisions.

bad, difficult, early, easy, likely, particular, tired, uncomfortable, uneasy, unreasonable

Yes	No

— Do you find it 1) ________________ to concentrate?

— Do you sleep 2) ______________?

— Are you 3) ______________ to worry too much?

— Do you feel 4) ______________ in tunnels, undergrounds, lifts, etc.?

— Do you wake up 5) ____________ , 6) ________________ when you go to bed 7) ___________ ?

— Do you feel 8) ________________ self-conscious (gehemmt) when people watch you at work?

— Do you blush 9) ______________ ?

— Are you 10) ________________ frightened of falling ill?

Now answer the questions and tick *yes* or *no*. If you have answered most of the questions with *yes*, then enter the words you have inserted in the hidden word puzzle below and you'll find a piece of good advice.

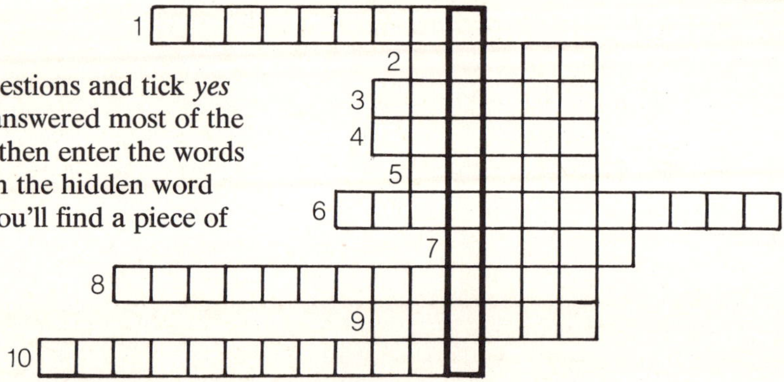

↑ hidden word

Position of Adverbs Exercise

Position of Adverbs

We have dealt with the formation and use of the adverbs, now there remains one final problem, namely their position in the sentence.

Would you perhaps like to test yourself to see if this is a problem for you at all? Put the adverbs given in brackets in their right position:

1. They bought a new house. (last year/in London)
2. It began to rain. (heavily)
3. I am tired of that job. (certainly)
4. He would have come. (never)
5. He has been loyal. (always)

Here is the solution have you got it right? If not, you may find the following rules helpful.

1. They bought a new house *in London last year*. 2. It began to rain *heavily*. 3. I am *certainly* tired of that job. 4. He would *never* have come. 5. He has *always* been loyal.

1. Adverbs of Manner
slowly, easily, badly, well, angrily, carefully, etc.

Adverbs of manner are usually placed after the verb. Sometimes, however, they may come before the verb or after the object.

Examples:

The sun was shining *brightly*. The birds were singing *happily*. She typed out the report *carefully*. She *carefully* typed out the report. They looked *angrily* at him. They looked at him *angrily*.

They	willingly gladly hurriedly happily	accepted her offer.

2. Adverbs of Place and Time
here, there, at school, in Munich, in the USA, etc.
yesterday, today, tomorrow, in 1845, next year, etc.

Adverbs of place and definite time are normally put at the end of a sentence. If you want to stress them, you can put them at the very beginning. If you have both in one sentence, the order is *place* before *time!*

↓ p *comes before* t ↓
in the alphabet

Adverbs
Position of Adverbs

Examples:
I met him *yesterday*. I didn't go on holiday *last year*. Will you see him *tomorrow?* I came here *in 1975. In 1975,* we moved to this place.

He emigrated to *Australia*. I went *to school in a small town in the countryside.* I went to *Moscow in 1973. In Moscow,* I met Boris.

If there are several adverbs of place or time, the most specific information is normally given first.

Examples:
They arrived at three o'clock in the morning on the second of January 1955. I live at 25, Hampshire Court, London.

3. Adverbs of Frequency
often, always, never*), seldom*), rarely*), sometimes, etc.

Adverbs of frequency normally go before the verb. If there are auxiliaries in the sentence, they go after the first auxiliary.
Sometimes, usually, normally can be put at the beginning of the sentence.

Dazu gibt es eine Eselsbrücke:
Hi Hi Vo Vo = Hinters Hilfsverb, vors Vollverb!

Examples:
He *always* gets up late. He is *always* late. I have *often* been there. They would *never* have come if they had known that. I don't *always* agree with you. *Sometimes,* I wonder what will become of him. I will *never* do that again.

4. Adverbs of Degree:
quite, rather, fairly, very, a bit, a little, etc.

Adverbs of degree precede the adjective or adverb they modify. A lot, a little, etc., sometimes modify a verb and can then be put after the verb.

Examples:
I know him *fairly* well. I am *very* pleased with my work. The music is *much too* loud. Could you turn it down *a little?* I felt *a little* sad when he told me that he couldn't come to the party.

---

*) For negative adverbs of frequency at the beginning of a sentence → p. 130.

Position of Adverbs Exercises

Exercise 8

Put the adverbs in brackets in their right position in the sentence.

1. Mrs. Thatcher and the Chinese leadership agreed to begin diplomatic negotiations on Hong Kong's future. (last week/in Peking)
2. He believed that they would not keep their promise. (strongly)
3. Two Southampton footballers will appear charged with rape. (on Tuesday/in a Swedish court)
4. I felt worried at what he said. (quite)
5. He has been to France. (often)
6. Our team played badly. (yesterday/in the match/at Leeds)
7. I have had enough to live on. (always)
8. I would have understood that if you hadn't explained it to me. (never/so patiently)
9. I don't understand what he says. (sometimes)
10. The train doesn't leave on time. (always)

Sometimes, there is a difference in meaning depending on the position of the adverb. Compare the following two sentences:

a) He wrote to her *foolishly*.
b) He *foolishly* wrote to her.

Can you see a difference between the two sentences, and if so, can you explain it?

Sentence a) means the *way* he wrote to her was foolish.
Sentence b) means that the *fact* that he wrote to her was foolish.

Now try to do the following exercise.

Exercise 9

Explain the difference in meaning.

1. a) He answered all my questions cleverly.
   b) He cleverly answered all my questions.
2. a) They planned to talk to him secretly.
   b) They secretly planned to talk to him.
3. a) She refused to talk to him sensibly.
   b) She sensibly refused to talk to him.
4. a) He couldn't explain it simply.
   b) He simply couldn't explain it.

Adverbs

Adverbs + Inversion

Adverbs + Inversion

Negative adverbs of frequency and other adverbs which express some sort of qualification (Einschränkung) are sometimes put at the beginning of a sentence for reasons of emphasis. If this is done, the so-called inversion becomes necessary. What exactly is inversion? Look at the following examples and try to find out.

I have never *seen* such a tall man.
= Never *have I seen* such a tall man.

I hardly *knew* him.
= Hardly *did I know* him, . . .

Inversion means that you do not follow the normal word order of a statement, but that you use the word order of a question. That means that you have to use *do/does/did* if there is no auxiliary in the sentence, just as you would in a normal question.

If you use this word order, you make your statements sound more formal.

Adverbs often used in that structure are:
never, seldom, scarcely ever, rarely, hardly, no sooner, under no circumstances, on no account, not until, not only, neither, nor, etc.

Exercise 10
Rewrite the following sentences by putting the adverbs underlined at the beginning of the sentence and make the necessary changes.

1. We hardly ever see them anymore.
2. I never had any trouble with him.
3. He little knows or cares what may happen.
4. He seldom changed a decision he had made.
5. I have rarely seen such a beautiful sight.
6. They scarcely ever experienced such difficult times.
7. He had no sooner arrived than he wanted to leave again.
8. I didn't believe that story for one moment. Not for . . .
9. The machine should under no circumstances be operated by an unskilled worker.
10. He didn't realize his mistake until many weeks later. Not until . . .

Adverbs + Inversion Exercise
In Addition "auch"

In Addition: auch

The German adverb auch and its equivalents in English.

There are several possibilities to render auch in English. They depend on whether you make a positive or a negative statement.

> For positive sentences use: also, too, as well.
> For negative sentences use: neither, nor, not . . . either.

Look at the following examples:

I prefer tea to coffee.	Ich auch:	I also prefer tea. I prefer tea too. I prefer tea as well. So do I.
(In colloquial English you can say:		Me too.)
I don't like coffee.	Ich auch nicht:	I don't like coffee either. Neither do I. Nor do I.
(In colloquial English you can say:		Nor me. Me either.)

Adverbs
In Addition "auch" Exercises

Exercise 11

Complete the following sentences. Mind the tenses!

Examples:
I love the opera, __________ my colleague.
I love the opera, and so does my colleague.
I don't like jazz, __________ my husband.
I don't like jazz, neither does my husband.

1. I hate bad TV programmes, ______________ my family.
2. I didn't go to school yesterday, ______________ Mary.
3. He won't come to your party, ______________ I.
4. When I asked him about that matter, he said he hadn't known anything about it, ______________ his wife.
5. The trade unions didn't want to give in, ______________ the management.
6. I will be out tomorrow evening, ______________ my parents.
7. Jane has passed the examination, ______________ Rosemary.
8. The parents were very pious (fromm), ______________ the children.

Exercise 12

Now use the form not . . . either.

Examples:
"I don't like jazz." — "I don't like it either."
He doesn't speak Russian. — She doesn't speak Russian either.

1. They don't want to do the work. — We . . .
2. The accused didn't tell the truth. — The witnesses . . .
3. The French government won't agree to that. — The English . . .
4. "I wouldn't do that if I were him." — "I . . .
5. "I don't like modern art." — "We . . .
6. Bob hasn't written so far. — Mary . . .

The Plain Truth about Plains and Planes

"Plain truth" is simple truth, "plains" refers to a geographical area (= Ebene, e. g.: The Great Plains of the Midwest) and "planes" are flat surfaces used in geometry or the plastic arts.

This chapter has little to do with the above words or even with airplanes. It is plainly about the more or less flat areas under our feet, which, unfortunately, seem to cause lots of problems.

Do you know when to use:	SOIL GROUND FLOOR
without mixing them up?	

If you are not sure, keep on reading.
If you look up the word Boden in a German-English dictionary you will immediately see the problem: it means all of those words above.
However in English those words are used to mean different things. And it is just as unlikely for a farmer to plow *(Am. E.;* plough = *Br. E.)* his floor as you would wash the soil of your living room. Nonsense, of course.

SOIL is of great interest to farmers and gardeners. Seeds or seedlings are planted in the soil. In some countries the soil has to be enriched with fertilizer or manure. Since the Black Power movement in the U. S. A. in the 1960s, many other ethnic groups have shown great interest in their original ancestral soil (= here soil is used figuratively and is equivalent to Heimat).

You can see from the examples that soil means the top covering or layer of earth and is used most often in connection with growing things. It is a synonym for earth (Erde oder, wie im letzten Beispiel, Heimaterde).

Before going on to the next two words we had better clear up a minor problem first. Namely, when do we use *earth* and *Earth.* The easiest rule is that we use non-capitalized earth to mean soil or where we live.
He stood outdoors, smelling the good earth he would soon plant with corn.
The astronauts came back from space and landed on earth.
He was sure he was the happiest man on earth .
Naturally, only the first example would be an synonym for soil.
Earth is only used when one is talking about the planets, one of which is the Earth. More than four billion people live on the planet Earth.

We think the best way to keep *ground* and *floor* apart is to think of ground as something outdoors and floor as something indoors.

The Plain Truth about Plains and Planes

The rain fell to the ground.

The ground shook and swayed during the Alaskan earthquake.

He dropped his cigar on the floor and burned a hole in the carpet.

She saw some beautiful parquet floors while in France.

And just another small digression. CARPET and RUG are both made of heavy material to cover floors. A carpet is larger than a rug. Some people put rugs on top of their carpets. Perhaps your living room has a wall-to-wall carpet? Maybe you have a thick rug next to your bath-tub?

Plains and Planes Exercises

Exercise 1
Fill in *ground, floor* or *soil.*

1. You'll never get that rocket off the ________________ !
2. I think wooden ________________ are prettier than concrete ones.
3. The chandelier came crashing to the ________________ .
4. The satellite came crashing to the ________________ .
5. What kind of ________________ is suitable for planting hops?
6. Standing outside in the storm, she could feel the ________________ shaking under her feet.
7. There is enough ________________ here to build a small apartment house.

Exercise 2
Fill in *earth* or *Earth.*

1. We have to push lots of ________________ in front of the dam.
2. The astronauts, looking back at the ________________ , saw a wonderful sight.
3. What planets, besides the ________________ , have moons?
4. Did you know that the ________________ weighs 66 sextillon (6.6×10^{21}) tons?
5. This ________________ is free of rocks and large amounts of clay.
6. In winter some animals burrow into the ________________ and sleep.
7. I am proud to be a citizen of this ________________ .

Conjunctions

How to Be Logical

This section will deal with conjunctions, i.e., with words you use to link two or more sentences. Of course it is quite impossible to deal with all of them here, but we will show you how to use the most important ones.

Concession Clauses

Concession clauses link two contrasting ideas. That is why it would perhaps be better to call them contrast clauses. Look at the following example:

His lecture was very boring, but I stayed till the end.

But is one of the conjunctions you can use to express such contrasting ideas. Can you think of other words? Try to find as many as you can to fit either in sentence A or B.

A His lecture was very boring, ________________ I stayed till the end.

B ________________ his lecture was very boring, I stayed till the end.

It is amazing how many possibilities there are to link contrasting ideas. It could lead you to a philosophical speculation that it seems to be man's main task to unite contrasting ideas! But this is not our task in hand. Here are the words you could have used in the above sentences:

Sentence A:	nevertheless, yet, however, still
Sentence B:	although, though, even though, despite the fact, in spite of the fact

All of them are interchangeable, but some carry more stress than others, e.g., *nevertheless* and *even though. Despite the fact* and *in spite of the fact* are more formal than the others.

Students often make mistakes with *despite* and *in spite of.*
Note the following:

1. There is no preposition after *despite!*
2. You always use *of* after *in spite,* which cannot be spelt as one word!
3. Both are always followed by a noun or gerund:
   Despite his high salary, he never managed to make ends meet.
   In spite of government subsidies, industry is not very willing to employ handicapped people.
4. When you use them as conjunctions, you have to add *the fact that* as can be seen in the examples above.

There are three more conjunctions in this category which we would like to bring to your attention.

Concession Clauses
Exercise

even if: combines the ideas of condition and contrast*), e. g.:

Even if the government was able to reconcile the disputing parties, the strike will have severe consequences on the nation's economy.

Even if you don't like rock music, you will enjoy this concert.

whereas: is a conjunction used to make a comparison by contrasting two things:

In English you never put a comma before *that,* whereas there is always one before daß in German.

while: besides having a temporal component, it is used

1. synonymously with *whereas:*
   While their country has plenty of natural resources, ours has none.
2. synonymously with *although:*
   While I understand your way of arguing, I can't agree with you.

Exercise 1

Use the following conjunctions in the sentences below. Give for each sentence as many variants as possible.

although, but, despite (the fact), even if, even though, however, in spite of (the fact), still, though, whereas, while, yet

1. He was certainly right, ________________ he should have given in for peace' sake.

2. ________________ they knew that the war was lost, they continued to fight.

3. English is easy at the beginning and becomes more and more difficult, ________________ most other languages are difficult at first and then become easier.

---

*) → 3. Conditional Clauses p. 143.

4. She seemed not particularly well suited for the job, ______ she got it because she was good-looking and had pleasant manners.

5. ______ the immense hopes that we had placed on it, our civilisation has failed to develop men of intelligence and culture who are capable of guiding us.

6. ______ you take every conceivable safety precaution, you may find yourself involved in an accident one day.

Exercise 2

Connect the following sentences by using one of these conjunctions:

although, but, even if, even though, whereas, while, yet.

Use each conjunction only once.

What have we done to our world!

1. There is a worldwide paper shortage. We throw away our old newspapers instead of recycling them.
2. Millions of people are starving. We live in greater prosperity than ever before.
3. Our air is polluted and our forests are dying. Industry continues to puff dangerous substances into the air.
4. Scientists tell us again and again that nuclear power stations are dangerous. We build them all the same.
5. We know that there is a tremendous overkill. We go on and produce more weapons.

Translating 'although', 'while' Exercise

6. We know that it is five minutes to twelve. We carry on as if we had all the time in the world.
7. ________________ we had the power to put an end to all the misuses immediately, we could not turn the clock back!

Hier möchten wir einen kurzen Ausflug ins Gebiet der Übersetzung einschalten. Da in vielen Examen eine Version verlangt wird, haben wir am Ende des Buches diesem Problem ein kurzes Kapitel gewidmet, in dem wir eine Musterübersetzung bieten mit ausführlichen Erläuterungen. Im Zusammenhang mit den Konjunktionen *although, though, even though, whereas* und *while* möchten wir jedoch schon an dieser Stelle darauf hinweisen, daß es neben den Übersetzungen mit *obwohl, wohingegen* und *während* noch eine andere Lösung gibt, die von Studierenden viel zu selten verwendet wird. Es ist die Übersetzung mit *zwar* oder *wenn auch,* die im Deutschen häufig viel besser klingt als die wörtliche Wiedergabe mit *obwohl* etc.*) Hier ein Beispiel:

Although he is very rich, he is not happy.
Obwohl er sehr reich ist, ist er nicht glücklich.
= Er ist zwar sehr reich, aber nicht glücklich.

= Wenn er auch sehr reich ist, so ist er doch nicht glücklich.

Im obigen Satz ist eine Übersetzung mit *obwohl* zwar möglich, aber man wird doch zugeben müssen, daß die beiden anderen Vorschläge wesentlich besser sind. Die Übersetzung mit *zwar* wird vor allem dann wichtig, wenn zwei Konjunktionen im Englischen zusammenkommen, etwa *that though, that while, because while,* etc.
Auch hierzu ein Beispiel:

I was told that, while he was no genius, he was a reliable worker.
Man sagte mir, daß er, obwohl (er) kein Genie (sei), ein zuverlässiger Arbeiter sei.
= Man sagte mir, er sei zwar kein Genie, aber doch ein zuverlässiger Arbeiter.

Daß hier die zweite Lösung unvergleichlich besser ist, wird wohl niemand bestreiten.

---

*) Dieses Problem wird ausführlich behandelt in dem Buch von Wolf Friederich "Technik des Übersetzens — Englisch und Deutsch". Dort finden sich viele interessante Beispiele mit Übersetzungen.

Conjunctions
Reason Clauses

Exercise 3

Please translate the following sentences into German using constructions with zwar or wenn auch.

1. While TV has the wonderful capacity to inform and entertain, you may question how it influences your child in other ways.
2. Although scientists are convinced that children can learn aggressive behaviour from TV, they are also sure that parents can reduce some of those effects.
3. Nobody dreams of prohibiting the use of tobacco or allowing the use of psychedelic drugs, whereas the problem of combatting drunkenness is one on which people are divided.
4. While many alternatives have been proposed for reforming the control of the press, no acceptable formula has yet been devised.
5. It will be our task to show that, although these circumstances were to a certain extent the factors which led to the disaster, they were not the genuine reason for it.
6. Most people would agree that, although our age far surpasses all previous ages in knowledge, there has been no corresponding increase in wisdom.

Reason Clauses

In exams you often have to answer questions on the text. Many of them begin with *why*. Your answers should then contain the word *because*. There is a rule — which is often broken — that you should not start your sentences with *because*. In colloquial English it is quite normal to begin with *because*, but in your written work you had better repeat part of the question so as not to irritate strict grammarians. Look at the following text and try to answer the two questions.

It may seem strange that language teaching in schools seems to be actually or at least proportionately and qualitatively decreasing, in an age when millions of Europeans from one country have taken to holidaying in another, and when young people at school are increasingly helped to travel abroad and involve themselves in the problems of other countries. But that month in the youth hostels of Greece, or digging ditches in Yugoslavia, or painting houses in the Netherlands may not do much to add to the pupils' linguistic achievement once they have learnt to communicate in the most basic way over work and play, beer, bed and board.*)

1. Why is it strange that language teaching should decrease?
2. Why do young people not get so much linguistic benefit from a stay in a foreign country?

*) Abitur 1974/75 Baden-Württemberg

Reason Clauses
Exercise

Start your answers as follows:

1. It is strange that language teaching is decreasing, *because* . . .
2. Young people do not get so much linguistic benefit from a stay in a foreign country, *because* . . .

Do not look at the solutions immediately, try to formulate the answers yourself first. Now compare:

1. ________________ because in our time people travel a lot and especially young people are encouraged to go abroad.
2. ________________ because they resort to the most basic ways of communication such as sign language. If they speak the foreign language at all, they do not pay attention to grammatical forms, etc., because all they want is to communicate.

The second answer could be rephrased by starting the sentence with: *The reason* . . . But be careful! German students tend to use *that* after *the reason,* which is wrong! It is either followed by *for* or *why*. Look:

> ! *The reason why + clause:*
> The reason why young people do not get much linguistic benefit from a stay abroad is that they resort to the most basic ways of communication.

> ! *The reason for + noun (or pronoun) + gerund:*
> The reason for young people not getting . . .
> The reason for them not getting . . .

There are three more conjunctions which have to be mentioned here:

as, since, for

As and *since* can be put at the beginning of the sentence or can come after the main clause and are often interchangeable.
As/Since it was raining, he took an umbrella.
He took an umbrella, *as/since* it was raining.

However, *since* is used if you refer to something which is already known or which we know is true, e.g.:

Since he was of age, his parents couldn't stop him from moving out.

> ! *As* and *since* can both have a temporal meaning. So make sure that there is no ambiguity. If in doubt, use *because!*

For is never used at the beginning of a sentence. It is very formal and has a slightly different meaning from *as, because* and *since.* It corresponds to the German conjunction denn and often gives an additional piece of information, or explanation, e.g.:

It is unwise to raise wages every year, *for* rising wages mean rising prices.

For can always be replaced by *because,* but then your sentence is less formal.

Exercise 4

Connect the following sentences by putting in

as, because, for, since, why

1. The army should be reduced in numbers, ______________ possession of large armies has led nations to war.
2. Students often have to answer questions on a text. This is the reason ______________ we are dealing with conjunctions like *because* here.
3. For Germans English is not very difficult at the beginning, ______________ there are many similar words.
4. It is vitally important that we save our forests from dying, ______________ their destruction has serious consequences not only for the quality of our air but for our water supply as well.
5. We stopped at a filling station ______________ we were running out of gas (= *Am. E.;* petrol = *Br. E.).*
6. A journalist should be careful to pass on information unchanged, ______________ truth is a delicate matter and should be handled with great care.
7. Why are you changing your clothes? — ______________ I'm going out.
8. Everyone knew that, ______________ the negotiations had failed, there was going to be a strike the next day.

Conditional Clauses

Conditional Clauses

It is quite surprising that, although there is a very simple, hard and fast rule for conditional clauses, students often make mistakes here — probably due to German interference. The rule is:

> ❗ Never use *will, shall, would* or *should* in a conditional clause!

If you stick to this rule, you'll always be on the safe side. (Although there are cases when you could use one of the above words in an if-clause, they do not pertain to formal written work.)

Conditional clauses can be introduced by

if, in case, provided, unless

and have a very strict sequence of tenses. There are three basic types:

	if-clause	main clause
Type 1	*present*	*future/imperative*
	If you want to come tonight,	I will*) stay at home. give me a ring.
Type 2	*past*	*conditional I*
	If they won the elections, If I were**) you,	we would*) be very worried. I wouldn't do that.
Type 3	*past perfect*	*conditional II*
	If he had tried to blackmail her,	she would have gone to the police.

By the way, the if-clause may either come at the beginning or at the end of a sentence. If it is at the beginning, it may be *followed* by a comma. But there is *no* comma *before* if!

There are some variations of the above rules:

1. Sometimes the main clause does not have a future idea in Type 1. Then you use the simple present, e. g.:

---

*) *shall/should* would be possible for the first person *(I, we)*, but with all the other persons *(you, he, she, it, they)* you have to use *will/would!*

**) Where is preferred to was.

Conjunctions
Conditional Clauses Exercise

In a multiple-choice-test you get several answers to a question, but only one is correct. So if a) is right, b) is necessarily wrong. If you heat metals, they expand.

2. Types 2 and 3 are sometimes combined, especially when the word *now* is used in the main clause, e.g.:

If I had been born a hundred years ago, I would probably be dead now. If he hadn't gambled away all his money, he would be quite rich.

Exercise 5

Put the verbs in brackets in their correct form.

1. If he (not exceed) the speed limit, he wouldn't have been fined.
2. If you want to translate Meinung into English, (not use) *meaning* but *opinion!*
3. If the public is prepared to accept trash in place of truth, then it (be) only natural that a commercial undertaking such as a newspaper should give the public what it wants.
4. What would you do if you (be) me?
5. If he hadn't been sure that they were honest people he (not get) involved in the deal.
6. Unless you remind him again, he (forget).
7. Provided you all (agree), we shall postpone the meeting.
8. Take a coat, in case it (rain).
9. If you go on drinking at that rate, you (be) drunk soon.
10. They (be) happier now if they had not married. But when they first met they thought they would die if they (not marry).
11. Some people say that if you gave people food, shelter, work and enough money, there (not be) any criminals.
12. If I (have) the choice, I'd rather live in a southern country.
13. The parties wouldn't have come to an agreement if they (not be forced) to by public opinion.
14. If you (listen) to the news regularly you would be better informed.
15. I'll leave immediately if you (start) talking about politics.

Color-ful Words: Words and Expressions Based on Colors

Words and Expressions Based on Colors

YELLOW: **He's yellow.** = He's a coward. (Feigling)
You can see the **yellow stripe down his back.**

RED: **He's a red.** = He's a communist or leftist.
He heard her remark and turned **red as a beet.** = He was embarrassed. (verlegen)
I wouldn't give you a **red cent** for that junk (= roter Heller).

If you want money from the government, you'll have to go through a lot of **red tape.** = bureaucratic rules and regulations often delaying and frustrating the requests of citizens.

The shoplifter was caught **red-handed.** = a thief caught in the act of stealing.

A **red-letter day** = a very important day. (Formerly, holidays were marked in red on church calendars.)

BLUE: **He's blue.** = sad, depressed (traurig, deprimiert). He's **got the blues.**
He's got **blue blood.** = noble family (blaues Blut).
She's a **bluestocking.** = a woman thought to be over-educated or intellectual. (Blaustrumpf)
A man who murders one wife after another is called a **bluebeard.**
= Named after Bluebeard, a fairy-tale character.

SILVER: Every cloud has a **silver lining.** = There's something good to be found in every experience, even the bad experiences one has.
That child was **born with a silver spoon in his mouth.** = Had all the advantages of wealth and comfort since birth.

GREEN: **She's got a green thumb.** = Naturally talented with plants and flowers. Everything grows nicely under her care.
When they saw the neighbors' (= *Am. E.*; neighbours' = *Br. E.*) new car they turned **green with envy.** = very envious (neidisch)
Greenbacks = American money (all bills – Geldscheine – are green.)

Color-ful Words: Words and Expressions Based on Colors

PINK: **In the pink** = in good health. I saw Jack last week and he was in the pink.
Tickled pink = very amused or happy. Jack was tickled pink by the news.
Pink (pinko) = having socialist leanings (a person supporting socialist or communist causes or ideas). Derogatory usage.

BLACK: **In the black** not in debt, solvent (opposite of being *in the red).* We've worked and worked and now finally this business is in the black. (Some banks print statements with credits in black and debits in red.)
The pot calling the kettle black. (Old saying) = to criticize someone else for the faults one has as well. (Ein Esel schimpft den anderen Langohr.)
black sheep = the bad, embarrassing member of a group, as in: She was the black sheep of the family because she did not join the family business.

WHITE: **white-collar worker** = office worker (as opposed to a blue-collar worker = manual worker; recently, pink collar worker = female worker). Refers to standard clothes worn in an office: jacket, white shirt and tie.
white lie = a harmless lie but somewhat stronger than an excuse.
whitewash = in politics, especially, to try to cover up or conceal or make harmless some serious misdeed. The politician tried to whitewash the money taken from big industry.
white elephant = something expensive to keep or maintain that has lost its value to the owner. The government is embarrassed by the many white elephants purchased by the military.

GOLD: **all that glitters/sparkles/glistens is not gold** = appearances can be deceptive; things are not always as good as they first may seem.
silence is golden = it is better to be quiet than to speak. (Sometimes in connection with the saying: **Talk is cheap** or **silence is golden, but speech is silver.**)

Color Idioms Exercises

Exercise 1

Fill in the blanks with a suitable **color** expression:

1. The store detective caught her ______________ ; she was actually stuffing little bottles of perfume into her boot.
2. They said he was __________ because he didn't want to join the army.
3. I just don't know how she does it. The soil is the same in her garden and just look how wonderfully her flowers are doing. She must have a ______________ . Sometimes, it just makes me turn __________ (with envy) when I see them.
4. Look at him. He looks so sad. He's been so ________ ever since his wife left him.
5. This is ridiculous. The government wants to know every little thing about our business. Getting through all the __________ is enough to make you quit trying to get a loan.
6. Oh, cheer up. It's not that bad. Every cloud has a __________ lining.
7. I know, but I get so mad. They won't give us a ______________ without us having to fill out a long form.

Exercise 2

Match the color with its meaning	
1. blue	A. socialist
2. green	B. cowardly feige
3. pink	C. sad
4. red	D. dear
5. yellow	E. communist
6. gold	F. envious neidisch

Bits & Pieces

Pronunciation Tip: words beginning with *au–* such as August, autumn, Austria, Australia & auction, etc., have the same pronunciation as words beginning with *aw-* such as awful, awesome & awe. It is not like the German *au,* which is pronounced like English *ou* as in "Ouch, that hurts!" or "Don't put your feet on my new couch!" or "Look, there's a cowboy!" (Now you read the paragraph above out loud, O.K.?)

An American Education
Schools in the U.S.A.*)

Both of my parents had to work, so when I was three years old I was brought to an all-day nursery school. Most of the time we played outdoors on swings and slides, building forts out of old tires, and swimming. We were given lunch there and afterwards we were supposed to take naps but I could never sleep and thus never got the candies that were laid on the beds of the children whose eyes were tightly closed, pretending to be asleep.

At five I went to kindergarten which was part of the elementary school, Hobart Blvd. School, named after the street it was on. I never learned who Hobart was,

though he must have been important because otherwise streets in America are named after numbers or letters or famous place names: meet you at the corner of Kentucky and 4th Street.

Elementary school went to the sixth grade and then I "graduated" to Virgil Junior High School, also named after the street. I joined the school band and we practiced every morning in first period – the day at school had seven periods.

During the lunch break there was also a record dance in the gymnasium for those who could eat quickly. Besides history, mathematics and English, we took gym, wood shop, plastic shop, electric shop, metal shop and drafting or industrial drawing. Remember, this was a public school and everyone had to go.
Well, after one year I transferred to a parochial school, St. Brendan's, which was not named after a street. We had eight periods and no band and no shops. We went to church a lot, though. And we spent a lot of time preparing for the entrance examinations to the parochial high schools. We took lots of practice exams in class and I learned that "I stand corrected" is a proper English sentence, at least on exams.

---

*) Try to read through this text without a dictionary. See if you can understand the meanings of the difficult words from the context. Definitions and explanations are given at the end.

Schools in the U.S.A.

Having done well on the exams, I enrolled at St. John Vianney High School — later named Daniel Murphy Memorial High School — neither of which had anything to do with the names of streets. The school band met during the lunch break and I played on the football team and track team after school. I had to take Latin and Classical Greek, biology, algebra, English, world history, religion and that was enough. I had plenty of homework and the teachers were very strict.

In high school, grade point averages (g.p.a.) were very important because they were a determining factor in getting into a good college or university. In America grades were A, B, C, D and F; F was fail. Other factors were the national college entrance examinations, Scholastic Aptitude Tests (S.A.T.), teacher recommendations, writing samples and personal interviews conducted by the colleges. Extracurricular activities such as sports, music, school newspapers, etc., were also taken into consideration. If you were a star basketball player, one could say that some universities also took grades into consideration.

I applied and was accepted by Claremont Men's College in California. The historian, Golo Mann, once taught there. I attended lectures and seminars and decided to major in history. Home was not far away, so I visited my mother and father, bringing along my laundry to be washed. There was an awful lot of studying to be done and many of my classmates flunked out of school within the first year; as soon as your g.p.a. got below a certain level, you were out. I registered for five classes each semester and each one had tests and term papers and sometimes oral reports.

Although I received a large scholarship, college was expensive. It was a residence college, meaning we lived and ate on campus. At the time, tuition was close to $2000 a year, plus fees, books and, of course, room and board, thus I figure college cost close to $5000 a year. That was in the '60 and now $10,000 tuition a year is not uncommon at U.S. schools. Most students financed their education by milking their parents, taking out loans and working in their "spare" time. At my college most of the gardeners, cafeteria workers and library pages were students.

It is unusual for undergraduates to take more than eight semesters to graduate, partly because of the costs involved, but mostly because of the careful control of grades each semester. Upon graduation I was awarded a Bachelor of Arts degree (B.A.) and then went on to graduate school to work for an M. A. and a Ph. D. You cannot just enter a university and head straight for a doctoral degree. You have to be an alumnus of an accredited college or university.

An American Education
Vocabulary

nursery school: before kindergarten; supervised play for young children. Nursery also means Baumschule.

kindergarten: one year preparation for normal school, usually only half-day.

elementary school: also called primary school or even grammar school in the U.S.A., i.e., the first six to eight years of school, depending on whether or not there is a junior high school. In the U.S.A. all public schools are comprehensive schools (= Gesamtschulen).

junior high school: grades seven to nine, i.e., six semesters.

gymnasium: (= Turnhalle) a building for indoor sports, e.g., basketball, gymnastics.

to take gym: to take a class in some subject, in this case gym = sports.

everyone had to go: in most States school is compulsory to the age of 16—18.

parochial: in this case a Catholic school; parochial in this sense any school with a religious orientation.

parochial high school: also some private schools and boarding schools (Internat) required entrance examinations.

took exams: someone gives you an exam and you take it.

did well on exams: passed the exams with high marks.

enroll: register for classes; put your name on the roll = attendance list.

homework: school work to be done at home; housework = cleaning up the house.
Ich muß heute Abend lernen = I have to study tonight.

strict: (= streng); strong (= stark)

g.p.a.: (= Notendurchschnitt)

college & university: For all practical purposes the difference between a college & university is one of size, not quality (Cf. below, **accredited**). Usually, a university is made up of several colleges. Not all colleges are undergraduate, e.g., Harvard Medical College.

grades: marks; notes are in music. Grade also means class; as in: He started school in the first grade. The last class in high school is 12th grade.

applied: also, apply for a job; apply for a loan (= sich bewerben)

attend & visit: attend school, concerts, meetings, lectures, seminars;
visit Aunt Tilda, Rome, graves, etc., implies your relationship is that of a guest. Attend implies membership and close attention, so you do not visit your school until after you graduate.

Schools in the U.S.A. Vocabulary

major: (= Hauptfach); minor (= Nebenfach). She majored in political science with a minor in philosophy. "What's your major?" — "Physical Education."

classmates: fellow students.

flunked out: failed or got poor marks and thus dismissed from school (colloquial). To drop out is to leave voluntarily. To be expelled (= ausgeschlossen).

term papers: (term = semester) Longer essays or research papers (= Semesterarbeit).

oral reports: (= Referate)

scholarship: Money for undergraduates; fellowship for graduate students; grant for research work or post-graduate or post-doctoral studies; stipend is rare in this context and simply means pay or fixed wage.

campus: the grounds and buildings of a university, college or school.

tuition: the money paid to attend college or private school; Br. E. tuition, instruction or course of studies.

B. A.: = academic degree awarded after four years of undergraduate liberal arts study and completion of all requirements. B. S. = Bachelor of Science. M. A. = Master of Arts (= Magister Artium). Ph. D. = Doctor of Philosophy (Dr. phil.).

alumnus: = male graduate of a college or university; pl. alumni; female: alumna; pl. alumnae; plural of male and female together = alumni.

accredited: recognized by various college associations setting minimum standards. The quality of the 3000 colleges and universities in the U.S.A. varies a great deal. By no means are the private schools "better" than the state universities, e.g., U.C. Berkely has been rated the top university in the U.S.A.; major difference is certainly the cost of tuition.

A Prescription for Picture Description

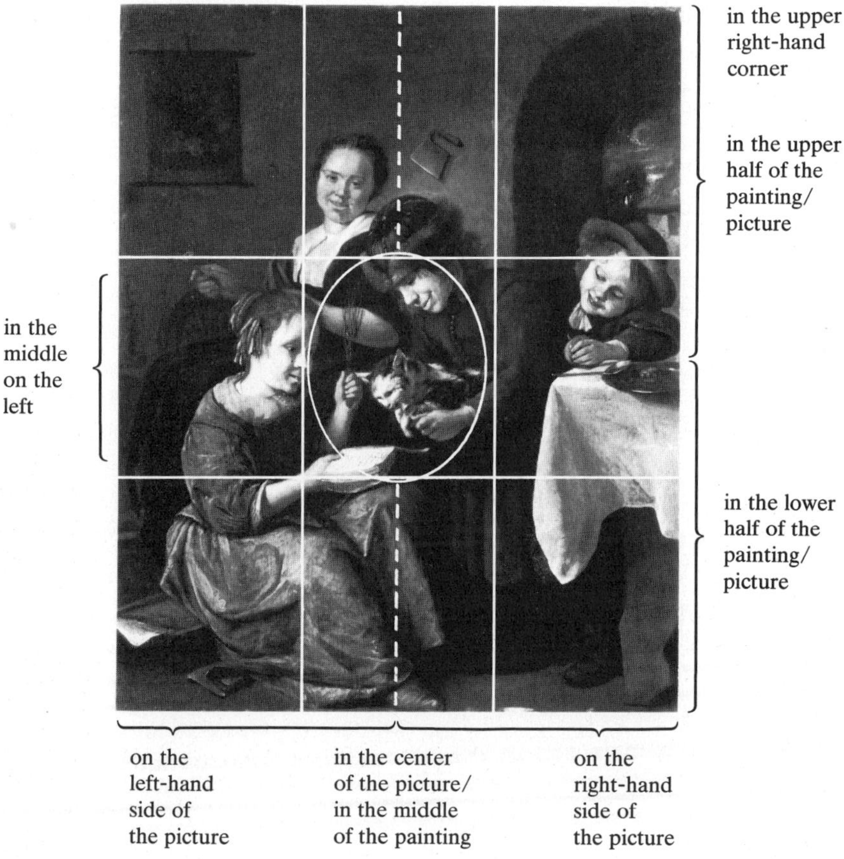

The cat is in the very center of the picture. The girl sitting on the left is holding a book and . . . In the lower . . . In the upper . . . In the center . . . On the left . . . On the right . . . At the top . . . At the bottom . . .

After studying the picture and the phrases for location above have a look at the following approach to picture description:

The three phases are:

1. observe; 2. interpret; 3. speculate.

Bildbeschreibung

1. Observe: begin by making general observations for orientation, such as: It's a drawing, a painting, a photograph, a print, a cartoon, etc.
It's an indoor/outdoor scene. It's a landscape, a portrait, a group portrait, etc. It's in an office, a city, on a farm, in the country, in a living room, etc. (All these patterns will also give you time to focus on more detailed descriptions or anticipate questions.) Next: describe people and objects generally — how many, how old, how large; what the time is; where they are in relation to each other, i.e., nearness, distance, sitting, standing, etc; mood, atmosphere, attitudes, postures, etc.

2. Interpret: if you are not sure about what something is or what someone is doing, be sure to use phrases like: "I'm not sure", "Maybe", "Perhaps", "I don't know, but possibly . . .", "It looks as if they are a family, together in their living room, but...", "The woman in the back might be the children's mother, but she could also be their older sister or an aunt or the babysitter."

The cat is in the center (*Br. E.* = centre) of the picture, so it *must* be important (interpretive use of *must*). The children *are looking* at the cat and seem amused (actions described by using the present continuous — as if the activity were happening at the moment). The girl on the left in the foreground is holding a switch (= Rute) while the cat is looking at the book. The cat looks afraid. Maybe, it is scared it is going to be hit. The title of the painting is: Kinder bringen einer Katze das Lesen bei by Jan Steen (1626—1679). (The painting by Steen is of children: *by* = artist; *of* = subject of the picture; *from* = who donated the painting. A painting by, of and from Pablo Picasso is a self-portrait given to the museum by the artist himself.) Knowing the name of the painting, we can now see that the children are making a game of a real live situation. Perhaps Steen is commenting on the absurdity of learning or schooling, at least from the standpoint of the children. For them, education is associated with pain and fear, partly due to corporal punishment practiced in some schools. If the children are cruel, it is because they have been taught to be so.

3) Speculate: You might be asked: "What are the children saying?" Or: What do you think the cat is thinking?" — "If you make another mistake, I will hit you!" & "I can't wait till this lesson is over!"
If the father came home now he might say: "Leave that poor cat alone!"
Finally, what caption (= Bildunterschrift) would you give this picture? How about: "The Cat's Reading Lesson", "The Education of a Cat", "The Tutorial", "The Private Lesson", or a translation: "Children Teaching a Cat How to Read."

Translation

Bei vielen Examen wird eine Übersetzung ins Deutsche verlangt. Deshalb geben wir Ihnen einige Hinweise, wie Sie diese Aufgabe am besten lösen.

1. Lesen Sie zuerst den ganzen Text konzentriert durch, und versuchen Sie, ihn inhaltlich zu verstehen. Einzelne unbekannte Wörter sollten Sie dabei übergehen.
2. Übersetzen Sie dann sorgfältig Satz für Satz. Achten Sie dabei auch auf Kleinigkeiten, z. B.: Steht im Original Plural oder Singular, der bestimmte oder unbestimmte Artikel usw.? Versuchen Sie nun, unbekannte Wörter aus dem Zusammenhang zu verstehen.
3. Lesen Sie Ihre fertige Übersetzung noch einmal durch. Vergleichen Sie sie satzweise mit dem Original, um sicherzugehen, daß Sie nichts ausgelassen haben. Haben Sie die Überschrift übersetzt? Paßt sie zum Text? Stimmt die Zeichensetzung im Deutschen?

Nun können Sie diese Hinweise gleich in die Praxis umsetzen. Übersetzen Sie den nachstehenden Text. Vergleichen Sie ihn dann mit der Musterübersetzung. Die Anmerkungen finden Sie im Schlüssel.

Education for All

How many educated persons should there be? It is an old question which, in view of the exalted claims that have been made for education, ought perhaps to change its form. How many can there be? Nobody doubts that there should be as many as possible, but estimates of possibility range high and low, depending in every instance upon general theories which the speaker holds. A. H., assuming madness in the mind of anyone who would "behave as though all human beings were by nature the same", proceeds at once to the proposition that it is "fantastic and absurd to give all children the same abstract education". Human beings, he explains, "belong to a variety of widely different types." This last is true enough, but it does not mean that they lack a common nature. If no such common nature exists, then the word "education" as such loses its excuse for being. Men are alike and different, as M. once made clear when he said that if the first were not true we should be unable to distinguish them from animals and if the second were not true we should be unable to tell them apart.

Übersetzung

Education has to master sameness and difference no less than permanence and change. The job is hard, and there is no shortcut by way of denying our common nature. Knowledge of that is basic to all knowledge; it supplies the educator's first axiom: No human being should miss the education proper to human being.

Bildung[1] für alle[2]

Wieviele Gebildete[3] sollte es geben? Dies[4] ist eine alte Frage, die, in Anbetracht[5] der überaus hohen Ansprüche[6], die man[7] an die Bildung gestellt hat, vielleicht anders formuliert werden sollte.[8] Wieviele kann es eigentlich[9] geben? Niemand zweifelt daran, daß es so viele wie möglich[10] sein sollten, doch die Beurteilungen[11] dessen, was möglich ist[12], sind sehr unterschiedlich[13] und hängen jeweils[14] von den allgemeinen Theorien des Einzelnen ab.[15] A.H., der jeden für verrückt hält[16], der „so tut[17], als ob alle Menschen von Natur aus[18] gleich seien[19]", kommt von dieser Auffassung aus[20] sogleich zu der Feststellung[21], daß es „phantastisch[22] und absurd[23] sei[24], allen Kindern dieselbe theoretische[25] Bildung zuteil werden zu lassen[26]". Die Menschen, erklärt er, „gehören vielen äußerst unterschiedlichen[28] Typen an." Letzteres ist nur allzu wahr, doch heißt das nicht, daß ihnen eine gemeinsame Natur fehle[30]. Wenn solch eine gemeinsame Natur nämlich[31] nicht besteht, dann verliert das Wort „Bildung" als solches jegliche Daseinsberechtigung.[32] Die Menschen sind gleich und doch verschieden[33], wie M. einmal darlegte, als er sagte, daß wir sie[34] – wenn ersteres[35] nicht wahr wäre – nicht von den Tieren und – wenn letzteres nicht zuträfe[36] – nicht voneinander unterscheiden könnten. Bildung muß also[31] der Gleichheit und der Verschiedenheit gerecht werden[37] ebenso wie[38] der Kontinuität und der Veränderung[39]. Die Aufgabe[40] ist schwer, und sie wird nicht leichter[41] dadurch, daß wir unsere gemeinsame Natur leugnen. Das Wissen[42] darum ist Grundlage für alles wissen; es liefert uns das erste Axiom des Pädagogen[43]. Kein Mensch sollte die dem Menschsein gemäße Bildung entbehren müssen.[44]

eine Erfahrung machen = **to have an experience.** The English-speaking mind sees experience as something that happens to you, thus you cannot "make" it, i. e., you cannot actively create or produce it, but you can put yourself in a position to have more experience, as in: I took the job to *gain* experience in accounting. Here, experience means knowledge or skill. The German idea of: Wir gingen nach Afrika um Erfahrungen zu machen is closer to the English idea of having exciting experiences, to be where interesting events take place, to see things in order to gain knowledge. Again, to gain or gather experience is in the realm of training.

I went to Disneyland and had many wonderful experiences meeting foreigners. She had an experience she will never forget. It all started on a motorcycle. Working at the bank, she gained much experience for her later career.

German Adopted English Which Is not English

Liliput, Liliputaner	from Swift's *Gulliver's Travels;* Engl: **Lilliputian;** often capitalized, but not always.
last not least	last *but* not least.
Smoking	Engl: smoking jacket = usually a fancy jacket worn only at home during the after-dinner hours; Smoking = formal suit, tuxedo.
hi-fi	**not** pronounced *"high fee";* it stands for high fidelity and is nonetheless pronounced: [ˌhaɪˈfaɪ]
Plaid	it is not used for Reisedecke; (plaid is a Scottish article of clothing, especially the national costume — we doubt they would appreciate hearing they were wearing a travel blanket.)
Mister	A man you do not know is not called 'Mister', but 'Sir'. Mister is sub-standard, for women say: Madam or Ma'am, not Lady.
Ami	for American, unknown outside of the German-speaking countries.
Silvester	unknown or very rare; = New Year's Eve.
life band/life show	obviously a mispronunciation of *live;* a live band as opposed to recorded music; life = Leben.

Key to Exercises

Pages 16–41

Miscellany of Confounded Words

Exercise 1

a. was robbed; b. were stolen; c. was robbed; d. was stolen; e. were stolen; f. were robbed; g. were stolen; h. was stolen; i. was stolen; j. were robbed.

Exercise 2

1. W; 2. C; 3. C; 4. W.; 5. W; 6. W; 7. C; 8. W; 9. W; 10. W; 11 C.; 12. W.; 13. W; 14. C; 15. C or W; 16. W; 17. C; 18 W; 19. W; 20. W; 21. W or C; 22. C; 23. W; 24. W.

Exercise 3

1. bench/bank; 2. noticed/remarks/remarked; 3. comfortable/convenient; 4. embarrassed/blamed; 5. floor/soil/ground; 6. naughty/angry/bad/evil; 7. fountains/well; 8. fat/thick; 9. engaged/committed/busy/involved; 10. remind/reminds/remember; 11. education/upbringing; 12. fault/mistake; 13. woman/wife/wives/women; 14. stories/history; 15. tall/large/great; 16. cards/map; 17. boil/cook; 18. control/check/check; 19. country/land; 20. have/let/leave; 21. lend/borrow; 22. loose/lose/loosen/loose/lose; 23. man/husband; 24. mean/opinion/think; 25. want/like; 26. news/message; 27. next/nearest/next/next/nearest; 28. fits/match/suits; 29. policy/politics/politics/policy; 30. robbed/steal/robbing/stole; 31. recipe/prescription; 32. told/says/tell/tell; 33. shadows/shade; 34 game/played/match; 35 votes/voice/voice/vote; 36. road/street; 37. technique/technology/technique; 38. bear/wear/carry; 39. choose/dial/elected/vote; 40 warehouse/department store.

Articles

Exercise 1

1. a, a; 2. an, a; 3. an; 4. a; 5. a, a, an; 6. an; 7. an.

Exercise 2

1. He is President of the United States; 2. He is a dentist; 3. She is Prime Minister of Great Britain; 4. He is a cook. 5. He is a conductor; 6. She is a waitress;

Exercise 3

1. a; 2. a; 3. —; 4. —; 5. —; 6. a; 7. a; 8. —; 9. a.

Exercise 4

Buckingham Palace, The Mall, Trafalgar Square, Charing Cross Road, Shaftsbury Avenue, Oxford Street, Bloomsbury Street

Exercise 5

1. the, —, —; 2. the; 3 —; 4. The; 5. —, the; 6. —, —; 7. —; 8. —, —; 9. the; 10. —, —; 11. —; 12. —, the; 13. —, the; 14. the; 15. —.

Nouns

Exercise 1

1. a slice of; 2. a bit of; 3. pieces of; 4. piece of; 5. bit of; 6. bit of; 7. pieces of; 8. bit of; 9. type *or* piece of/types *or* pieces of; 10. pieces of *or* lumps of; 11. piece of.

Exercise 2

They are all correct sentences except the last one. There verb and subject do not agree because news is singular, hence "The news has . . .".

Exercise 3

1. bacteria; 2. psychoses; 3. phenomena; 4. data; 5. children; 6. sheep; 7. crises; 8. dramas; 9. museums; 10. areas; 11. territories;

Key to Exercises

Pages 41–57

12. monkeys; 13. monies *or* moneys; 14. dogmas; 15. bases; 16. cows; 17. losses; 18. oases.

The Language of the Body

Exercise 2

1. his; 2. for; 3. leg/for; 4. her/her/her; 5. your.

Adjectives

Exercise 1

1. more bizarre; 2. friendlier; 3. more alone; 4. more worried; 5. shyer; 6. thinner; 7. cleverer; 8. simpler; 9. quieter and quieter; 10. more dead.

Exercise 2

```
            10
       1n e a r e s t
     2l a s t
    3f u r t h e r
     4l a t e s t
       5w o r s e
          6b e t t e r
  7s m a l l e r
     8l e s s
     9n e x t
```

Exercise 3

1. eldest; 2. older; 3. elder/eldest; 4. oldest; 5. elder.

Exercise 4

1. Russian is as difficult as Greek. 2. Your coffee is as good as my mother's coffee. 3. Teachers work as hard as students. 4. Cats are as intelligent as dogs. 5. Our living room is as large as our bedroom. 6. Skiing is as strenuous as skating.

Exercise 5

1. Russian isn't as/so difficult as Greek. 2. Your coffee isn't as/so good as my mother's coffee. 3. Teachers don't work as/so hard as students. 4. Cats aren't as/so intelligent as dogs. 5. Our living room isn't as/so large as our bedroom. 6. Skiing isn't as/so strenuous as skating.

Exercise 6

1B, 2I, 3E, 4A, 5C, 6D, 7H, 8F, 9K, 10L, 11J, 12G.

Exercise 7

1. He is better than his brother because he is more careful. 2. A Mercedes is faster than a Fiat because the engine is bigger. 3. Summer is nicer than winter, because it's warmer. 4. Robert is more successful than Peter because he works harder.

Exercise 8

1. the cheaper/better/more easily; 2. the less; 3. the thinner/better; 4. the more.

Exercise 9

1. as tall as, than; 2. and; 3. than; 4. as soon as; 5. than; 6. and; 7. than.

Exercise 10

Be careful that you use the present perfect "have met", etc., with *ever* throughout the exercise! (→ Tenses, p. 101)

1. Yes, she is the nicest woman I have ever met. 2. Yes, he is the best student I have ever had/known. 3. Yes, it was the worst accident I have ever had. 4. Yes, it (he/she) is the most intelligent dog I have ever had. 5. Yes, it was the most interesting play I have ever

Key to Exercises Pages 57–82

seen. 6. Yes, it was the most terrible/worst concert I have ever heard/been to.

Exercise 11
1. —; 2. man/woman; 3. —, —; 4. man; 5. topics; 6. thing; 7. —; 8. —, —; 9. element.

Exercise 12
1. one; 2. —; 3. ones; 4. (one); 5. (one) (one); 6. ones; 7. —.

Trip — Stumble — Fall

Exercise
1. advertising campaign; 2. current/topical; 3. avenue; 4. emergency ward; 5. circus performer; 6. became/artist; 7. got; 8. career; 9. boss; 10. Christian/Christianity; 11. notes; 12. (groups of) companies; 13. denomination; 14. consistent; 15. critique/critic/review; 16. soft/unobtrusive; 17. delicious; 18. uninterested; 19. disinterested; 20. perhaps/possibly; 21. awkward/disastrous; 22. parliamentary groups; 23. ingenious; 24. secondary school/grammar school/high school; 25. humane; 26. dinner/meal; 27. murderers/murder; 28. didn't hear; 29. guesthouse/boardinghouse; 30. photographer; 31. on principle/in principle; 32. brochure; 33. self-confident; 34. sensitive; 35. respectable; 36. rivers; 37. likable.

Discrimination and Prejudice

Exercise 1
prejudices/discriminated against/discrimination/prejudice about.

Exercise 2

R	A	C	I	S	T						
		P	R	E	J	U	D	I	C	E	
		B	E	G	G	A	R				
D	I	S	C	R	I	M	I	N	A	T	E
			R	E	B	E	L				
			A	G	A	I	N	S	T		
	A	T	T	A	C	K					
		H	A	T	E						
S	L	A	V	E							

Exercise 3

1 A	L	3 I	E	5 N	■	9 A
G	■	N	■	2 O	7 F	F
3 A	U	T	O	■	4 A	T
I	■	E	■	5/6 R	D	■
6 N	E	G	R	O	E	10 S
S	■	R	■	O	■	T
7 T	2 R	A	I	T	8 O	R
■	8 I	T	■	9 S	H	E
10 G	O	E	4 S	■	■	S
■	T	■	11 O	U	R	S

Gerunds = -ing forms

Exercise 1
1. No, there is no use writing to him. 2. No, it's no good telling her. 3. No, I wouldn't mind repeating it. 4. No, it wasn't worth getting into an argument. 5. No, I don't mind your sitting there. 6. No, I can't stand listening to it. 7. No, I can't help knowing it. 8. No, I can't bear hearing any more bad news.

Exercise 2
eating/to eat; watering/to water;
to wash/washing; painting/to paint

Key to Exercises

Pages 84–99

The Language of Money, Money

Exercise 1

1. economists; 2. economics; 3. economy; 4. economic; 5. economical; 6. economize; 7. save; 8. economic; 9. spare; 10. economical.

Exercise 2

A 9 / B 4 / C 10 / D 13 / E 2 / F 8 / G 1
H 7 / I 5 / J 11 / K 6 / L 3 / M 12 / N 14.

Tenses

Exercise 1

1. I'm going/are you going/I'm going/go; 2. I'm waiting/wait; 3. cook/I'm cooking; 4. is playing/plays/plays; 5. speak/is speaking; 6. Am I disturbing/disturb.

Exercise 2

1. meets; 2. is taking place; 3. is trying; 4. tries; 5. is rising; 6. rise; 7. are changing over; 8. boils; 9. is boiling; 10. are introducing.

Exercise 3

1. is losing; 2. are urging; 3. lies, are fighting; 4. comes, offers, means, get, provides; 5. burst, die off, depends; 6. are finding; 7. is considering; 8. are trying; 9. are spending.

Exercise 4

A 1. He is always borrowing money from me. 2. She is forever saying no when . . . 3. He is constantly complaining about . . . 4. Those children are asking silly questions all the time. 5. My mother is continually telling me . . . 6. He is constantly changing his mind.

B 1f, 2e, 3d, 4a, 5c, 6b.

Exercise 5

1. is watching, is looking through, is reading, is listening; 2. do you think, I think; 3. I am thinking (= now and constantly) *or* I think (= regularly); 4. didn't (couldn't) see or hear; 5. don't (can't) see; 6. is seeing; 7. Do you have; 8. is having; 9. was feeling for; 10. felt.

Exercise 6

1. a/b; 2. a/a; 3. b; 4. a; 5. a; 6. b; 7. a; 8. a *or* b; 9. a; 10. b.

Exercise 7

1. since; 2. for; 3. for; 4. since; 5. for; 6. since; 7. since; 8. Since.

Exercise 8

1. He has been in hospital since his accident./Since his accident . . .
2. I have been waiting for you for an hour. (Schon ist durch die continuous tense ausgedrückt.)
3. Since his divorce he has spent every evening in the club. He has spent . . . since his divorce.
4. I have had a new car for one week.
5. We have had awful weather since last month.
6. We have been living in Munich for several years.
7. I have known him for more than 10 years, and he has always been very reliable.
8. The strike of the steelworkers has already lasted (for) four weeks now.
9. I have been playing (have played) tennis for two years, but I don't really like (enjoy) it.
10. They have lived (have been living) in a house of their own (in their own house) for years.

Key to Exercises

Pages 102–111

Exercise 9

1. I have only recently begun; 2. Have you ever seen . . . No, I haven't, but I saw . . . 3. She was . . ., but she has been . . . 4. . . . we have been lucky . . . 5. Frank telephoned . . . 6. You have had . . . 7. I have just finished . . . 8. . . . I always bought . . . 9. Have you had . . . — I had . . . 10. has written *(D. Lessing is still alive)* 11. wrote *(O. Wilde is dead).*

Exercise 10

1. a, b, c; 2. b, a, c; 3. c, b, a; 4. c, b, a; 5. c, a, b; 6. a, b, c.

Exercise 11

2. He was appointed yesterday after . . . 3. The police stepped in and forced them to leave . . . The leaders were arrested. The others were taken to hospital. 4. This decision was announced yesterday after . . . 5. When the accident became known, an inquiry was started. The cans were returned and destroyed. 6. Mr. P. made the call at Athens last week. 7. They were involved in . . .

Exercise 12

1. were put; 2. has negotiated; 3. has been, arrived, started; 4. have joined, was found; 5. have died, broke out; 6. has been seized, was announced.

Exercise 13

1. bought, did you buy, dit it cost; 2. have you ever heard, lived, was; 3. I have lost, where you lost, Did you find, they were; 4. has written, wrote, was; 5. have you lived, have lived, I came, I lived.

Exercise 14

1. a) You state a fact. b) You stress the activity.
2. a) Now it's clean. You have finished.
   b) You are still at it, you haven't finished yet.
3. a) You are through with it. b) You are not quite through with it and don't know the result yet.

Exercise 15

1. have looked through . . . and sorted out . . . 2. have been looking through . . . haven't found it yet; 3. Have you finished, . . . I have been working at it . . . haven't finished yet. 4. have been trying/have tried . . . 5. have lived/have been living; 6. has been working . . .

Exercise 16

1. was talking, arrived, saw, put down; 2. left, put on, was raining; 3. left, was wearing; 4. got up, had, took, went out; 5. was getting up (war dabei aufzustehen), rang *oder* got up (stand auf), rang; 6. went; 7. was; 8. got, knew, were approaching; 9. did you do, read, Did you finish, told.

Exercise 17

A) went over, gave, was, danced*), were, came in*), were sitting, were, was playing, was working, was

B) felt, was falling, caught, was not looking, or thinking or talking, were, did not need, felt, was rushing, felt, was pulling, could, could, was looking.

* The author used *danced* and *came in* because he was describing a custom, something that happens every year on July 14!

Key to Exercises

Pages 113–125

Exercise 18
1. outraged, had already made; 2. had anticipated, came; 3. was killed, had been; 4. had been battered, was reached, left; 5. reacted; 6. had reacted.

Explanation p. 115
I'll see him tomorrow:
states an intention; probably said at the moment of decision
I'll be seeing him tomorrow:
is said to state a fact, but does not express the speaker's intention. "Anyway" could be added to the sentence.

Exercise 19
1. will go and see; 2. I'll be seeing; 3. I'll have; 4. I'll be running; 5. we'll be flying; 6. I'll not be/ I won't be; 7. will immediately commence.

Exercise 20
1. will be; 2. is going to break; 3. is going to fail; 4. will fail; 5. will presumably try; 6. is going to have; 7. will type 8. am going to write.

Exercise 21
1. falls; 2. is going to be opened; 3. am going; 4. will rise/are going to rise; 5. am flying/going to fly; 6. leaves.

Exercise 22
1. We'll need a new car soon. Our old one is almost falling apart. 2. We are going to buy a Mercedes this time. 3. I have heard that you want to emigrate. You will probably feel quite lonely at the beginning. 4. Tomorrow I am flying to Australia for six weeks. It is going to be (will be) a long journey, but they will be showing films during the flight to pass the time. 5. Christmas falls on a Sunday this year. 6. I hope he will come to our party. 7. He will (is going to) end up in prison (gaol) one day! 8. Tomorrow at this time I'll be lying on the beach. 9. I'm going to spend my next holiday in the mountains. 10. The course starts on May 15 and goes (runs) till June 4.

Adverbs

Exercise 1
1. systematically; 2. fully; 3. comfortably; 4. truly; 5. publicly; 6. noisily; 7. openly, not in such a cowardly manner; 8. shyly; 9. quickly, well

Exercise 2
1. silently; 2. curiously; 3. gracefully; 4. furiously; 5. patiently; 6. enthusiastically; 7. completely indifferently; 8. Politically; 9. Legally.

Exercise 3
1. He writes legibly. 2. We issue our report yearly. 3. She smiled at me in a friendly way. 4. He married early. 5. . . . she looked at me reproachfully. 6. He replied angrily. 7. She sighed deeply. 8. You have worked very well.

Exercise 4
1. much; 2. a lot of; 3. a long way; 4. far; 5. long; 6. a long time.

Exercise 5
1. earlier; 2. worse; 3. more sensibly; 4. least; 5. harder, less; 6. best; 7. better; 8. faster, more carefully; 9. politely.

Exercise 6
1. economic, extremely; 2. economically; 3. intelligent, clever; 4. incredible, tremendously; 5. conceivable, likely; 6. conceivably; 7. wonderful, delicious; 8. unbelievable; 9. unbelievably; 10. politically, necessarily, popular.

Key to Exercises Pages 126–135

Exercise 7

				1 d	i	f	f	i	c	u	l	t				
											2 b	a	d	l	y	
											3 l	i	k	e	l	y
											4 u	n	e	a	s	y

1 d i f f i c u l t
2 b a d l y
3 l i k e l y
4 u n e a s y
5 t i r e d
6 p a r t i c u l a r l y
7 e a r l y
8 u n c o m f o r t a b l y
9 e a s i l y
10 u n r e a s o n a b l y

Exercise 8

1. In Peking last week, Mrs. Thatcher . . . 2. He strongly believed . . . 3. . . . will appear in a Swedish court on Tuesday charged with rape *or* On Tuesday . . . will appear in a Swedish court . . . 4. I felt quite worried . . . 5. He has often been . . . 6. . . . played badly in the match at Leeds yesterday *or* Yesterday our team . . . in the match at Leeds. 7. I have always had . . . 8. I would never have understood . . . to me so patiently 9. Sometimes I don't . . . *or* I don't . . . sometimes. 10. . . . doesn't always leave . . .

Exercise 9

1. a) His answers were clever. b) It was clever of him to answer all my questions. 2. a) They wanted to talk to him without anybody knowing. b) They planned it in secret. 3. a) She didn't talk to him in a sensible way. b) It was sensible of her not to talk to him at all. 4. a) He couldn't find simple words, his explanation was too complicated. b) He couldn't explain it at all.

Exercise 10

1. Hardly ever do we see them anymore. 2. Never did I have any trouble with him. 3. Little does he know or care what may happen. 4. Seldom did he change a decision he had made. 5. Rarely have I seen such a beautiful sight. 6. Scarcely ever have they experienced such difficult times. 7. No sooner had he arrived than he wanted to leave again. 8. Not for one moment did I believe that story. 9. Under no circumstances should the machine be operated by an unskilled worker. 10. Not until many weeks later did he realize his mistake.

Exercise 11

1. and so does my family; 2. neither did Mary; 3. Neither (nor) will I; 4. neither (nor) had his wife; 5. neither (nor) did the management; 6. and so will my parents; 7. and so has Rosemary; 8. and so were the children.

Exercise 12

1. We don't want to do it either. 2. The witnesses didn't tell the truth either. 3. The English won't agree either. 4. I wouldn't do it either. 5. We don't like it either. 6. Mary hasn't written either.

The Plain Truth about Plains and Planes

Exercise 1

1. ground; 2. floors; 3. floor; 4. ground; 5. soil; 6. ground; 7. ground

Exercise 2

1. earth; 2. earth; 3. Earth; 4. Earth; 5. earth; 6. earth; 7. earth

Key to Exercises

Pages 137–147

Conjunctions

Exercise 1

1. but/nevertheless/however/yet/still; 2. Although/though/even though/despite the fact that/in spite of the fact that; 3. whereas/however/but/while; 4. but/nevertheless/yet/still/however; 5. Despite/In spite of; 6. Even if

Exercise 2

1. Although there is . . . we throw away . . . 2. Millions of people are starving whereas/while we live . . . 3. Our air is . . ., yet/but industry . . ./Although/Even though our air is polluted, industry . . . 4. Although/Even though scientists tell us . . ./Scientists tell us . . ., yet/but we build . . . 5. Even though/Although we know . . ./We know that there is a tremendous overkill, but/yet we go on . . . 6. Although/Even though we know . . ./We know . . . but/yet we carry on . . . 7. Even if we had the power . . .

Exercise 3

1. *Wenn* das Fernsehen *auch* die wunderbare Fähigkeit besitzt, zu informieren und zu unterhalten, so werden Sie sich vielleicht doch fragen, ob es nicht auch andere Einflüsse auf Ihr Kind ausübt. (Das Fernsehen hat *zwar* einerseits . . ., aber Sie werden sich andererseits doch auch fragen . . .)
2. Wissenschaftler sind *zwar* überzeugt, daß Kinder vom Fernsehen aggressives Verhalten lernen, sie sind aber auch sicher, daß Eltern diese Wirkungen teilweise (zum Teil) auffangen (mildern, abschwächen) können. 3. *Zwar* denkt niemand auch nur in Traum daran, den Genuß von Tabak zu verbieten oder den von psychedelischen Drogen zu erlauben (zuzulassen), doch beim Problem der Bekämpfung des Alkoholismus scheiden sich die Geister (ist man geteilter Meinung/gehen die Meinungen auseinander). 4. Man hat *zwar* viele Alternativen vorgeschlagen (Alternativvorschläge gemacht), um die Kontrolle (Überwachung) der Presse zu reformieren, doch ist bis jetzt keine annehmbare Formel entworfen worden. 5. Es wird unsere Aufgabe sein zu zeigen, daß diese Umstände *zwar* bis zu einem gewissen Grade die Faktoren waren, die zu dem Desaster führten, daß sie aber nicht der eigentliche Grund dafür waren. 6. Die meisten werden dem zustimmen (darin übereinstimmen), daß unser Zeitalter die früheren *zwar* an Wissen überflügelt hat (bei weitem übertrifft), daß es jedoch keinen entsprechenden Zuwachs an Weisheit gegeben hat.

Exercise 4

1. for (since, as, because); 2. why; 3. because (as, since); 4. since (as, because); 5. because; 6. for (because); 7. Because; 8. because;

Exercise 5

1. had not exceeded; 2. don't use; 3. is; 4. were; 5. would not have got; 6. will forget; 7. agree; 8. rains; 9. will be drunk; 10. would be, didn't marry; 11. wouldn't be; 12. had; 13. had not been forced; 14. listened; 15. start.

Color-ful Words

Exercise 1

1. red-handed; 2. yellow; 3. green thumb/green; 4. blue; 5. red tape; 6. silver; 7. red cent

Exercise 2

1 C / 2 F / 3 A / 4 E / 5 B / 6 D

Key to Exercises

Page 155

Translation *)

[1]Nach der Definition des „Dictionary of Contemporary English“ ist *education: (the results of) teaching or the training of mind and character.* Das entspricht im Deutschen dem, was wir unter Erziehung *und* Bildung verstehen. Da das Wort *education* im Text jedoch häufig vorkommt, wäre die Übersetzung mit dem Doppelbegriff schwerfällig. Man wird sich hier also für Bildung entscheiden müssen, wovon sich dann auch gut das Adjektiv gebildet für *educated* ableiten läßt. Der deutsche Begriff Erziehung allein ist nicht umfassend genug. Ausbildung wäre im Englischen *training* und ist hier nicht akzeptabel. Schulbildung ist möglich, aber Bildung ist besser.

[2] *oder:* für jedermann, für jeden

[3] Englische Adjektive können nicht ohne weiteres als Substantive verwendet werden (→ S. 58), daher muß hier im Englischen das Stützwort *persons* zu *educated* treten. Im Deutschen können wir hier *gebildete Menschen* sagen, müssen es aber nicht unbedingt.

[4] Die wörtliche Übersetzung (Es ist eine alte Frage) ist sicherlich möglich. Besser ist es allerdings, für es *das* oder *dies* zu setzen, weil dadurch der Bezug zum vorhergehenden Satz deutlicher wird, was der Vorliebe des Deutschen für klare Bezüge und erklärende Zusätze entgegenkommt.

*) Viele der übersetzerischen Probleme, die hier nur angetippt werden konnten, weil eine ausführliche Darstellung den Rahmen dieses Buches sprengen würde, sind eingehend behandelt in dem Buch von Wolf Friederich, *Technik des Übersetzens — Englisch und Deutsch,* Hueber Verlag, Ismaning, 1969.

[5] *oder:* angesichts

[6] *oder:* sehr hohen Anforderungen; *exalted* ist im Gegensatz zu dem deutschen Wort exaltiert nicht negativ! exaltiert = exaggerated; für Personen: over-excited.

[7] Das englische Passiv kann im Deutschen häufig mit *man* wiedergegeben werden. . . ., *die an die Bildung gestellt worden sind,* ist hier zwar denkbar, die Lösung mit *man* ist jedoch viel eleganter.

[8] *oder:* umformuliert/anders gestellt werden sollte. Alle Lösungen mit dem Substantiv Form (etwa: sollte vielleicht ihre Form ändern) klingen im Deutschen schwerfällig, ja sogar unlogisch.

[9] Man sollte nicht vergessen, daß wir im Deutschen häufig Füllwörter einfügen, die dem Englischen weitgehend unbekannt sind, und die als erklärende Zusätze dienen (→ Anm. 4 und 20).

[10] *oder:* möglichst viele

[11] *oder:* Einschätzungen

[12] Alle substantivischen Lösungen klingen im Deutschen merkwürdig (etwa: Möglichkeitseinschätzungen, Möglichkeitsbeurteilungen, Schätzungen der Möglichkeit). Denkbar wäre noch *die Beurteilung des Machbaren,* doch ist dem die Umschreibung mit einem Nebensatz vorzuziehen.

[13] *oder:* unterscheiden sich sehr voneinander/ gehen weit auseinander. *High and low* ist eine Redewendung, die entweder *hoch und niedrig* heißt oder *überall:* I looked for it high and low = ich habe überall danach gesucht. Hier heißt es, daß die Zahlen, die genannt werden, hoch und niedrig sind.

Key to Exercises

Page 155

[14] *oder:* in jedem einzelnen Fall
In jedem Fall sollte vermieden werden, um einer Verwechslung mit *auf jeden Fall* (= in any case) vorzubeugen.
eine weitere Möglichkeit: je nach den allgemeinen Theorien des Einzelnen.

[15] Die Lösung mit einem Nebensatz: . . ., *die der Sprecher hat,* ist wohl kaum denkbar. Möglich wäre noch: die jemand hat; die Version mit dem Genitiv (des Einzelnen/des Betreffenden/des Sprechenden) ist jedoch stilistisch besser.

[16] Auch hier ist die substantivische Lösung (Verrücktheit im Geiste eines jeden) zwar verständlich, Deutsch ist das aber nicht.

[17] behave = sich benehmen, verhalten
behave as if (though) = so tun, als ob
He behaves as if he were the boss. = Er tut so, als ob er der Chef sei.

[18] nicht: durch die Natur/in ihrer Natur!
Ähnliche Wendungen mit *by* sind: by profession = von Beruf; by training = der Ausbildung nach.

[19] In der Umgangssprache hört man hier oft „wäre". Da dies aber ein hochsprachlicher Text ist, sollte man auf jeden Fall den grammatikalisch richtigen Konjunktiv I setzen.

[20] proceed to = eigentlich: weitergehen/übergehen/schreiten zu; Diese Übersetzungen sind aber hier nicht brauchbar. Der Zusatz *von dieser Auffassung aus* ist zwar etwas deutlicher und ausführlicher als das englische *proceed,* wird dem aber doch noch am ehesten gerecht, vor allem wenn man bedenkt, daß das Deutsche erklärende Zusätze liebt (→ Anm. 4). Möglich wäre noch: kommt von daher sogleich . . .

[21] nicht: Vorschlag = proposal; Schluß = conclusion; Annahme = assumption

[22] *oder eventuell:* wirklichkeitsfremd/unrealistisch

[23] *oder eventuell:* unsinnig
Da jedoch im Deutschen sowohl *phantastisch* als auch *absurd* durchaus annehmbare Lösungen sind, besteht eigentlich keine Notwendigkeit, sie zu ersetzen.

[24] *oder:* ist

[25] „Abstrakte Bildung" erscheint mir im Deutschen keine übliche Formulierung. „Akademisch" bezieht sich nur auf Universitätsbildung!

[26] Im Deutschen kann man Bildung nicht geben, nur jemandem vermitteln oder angedeihen lassen, zwei Varianten, die hier auch möglich sind.

[27] *oder:* einer Vielzahl
Im Englischen steht häufig ein Substantiv, wo wir im Deutschen ein Adjektiv vorziehen: the coldness of the water = das kalte Wasser; your fairness of judgement = Ihre faire Beurteilung; a variety of goods = viele verschiedene Waren.

[28] *oder:* ganz verschiedenen/sehr unterschiedlichen

[29] *oder:* Diese letzte Aussage/Äußerung/Feststellung

[30] *oder:* daß sie keine gemeinsame Natur hätten/nichts Gemeinsames hätten. Auch Indiktativ: fehlt, haben, ist möglich.

[31] → Anm. 4, 9, 20

Key to Exercises Page 155

[32] *excuse* heißt unter anderem auch Rechtfertigung, Grund. Das geläufigste deutsche Wort ist Daseinsberechtigung. Alle Lösungen mit Entschuldigung etc. sind nicht akzeptabel.

[33] *oder:* gleichen und unterscheiden sich doch. Das *doch* ist hier geradezu unentbehrlich, → Anm. 4 und 9.

[34] Im Deutschen können zwei Konjunktionen nicht unmittelbar nacheinander stehen. (Im Englischen können sie nur nacheinander stehen!) Deshalb müssen wir erst mindestens das Subjekt des daß-Satzes bringen, (hier am besten auch noch das Objekt), ehe wir den Einschub anfügen können.

[35] *oder:* das erste – das zweite

[36] *oder:* wenn letzteres nicht wahr wäre
Da das Deutsche aber die Abwechslung liebt, ist eine Abwandlung vorzuziehen.

[37] *master* = eigentlich: *meistern;* aber im Deutschen kann man das nicht mit Verschiedenheit bzw. Gleichheit verbinden.

[38] *no less than* = eigentlich: *nicht weniger als;* klingt hier aber schwerfällig. Daher werden hier die beiden negativen Wörter „no“ + „less“ in ein positives = „ebenso“ verwandelt.

[39] *oder:* dem Bleibenden und dem sich Ändernden/dem Wandel/dem Wechsel

[40] *Job* kann hier auf keinen Fall mit *Job, Arbeit* oder *Beruf* übersetzt werden.

[41] Eine Definition für *shortcut* ist: a method of doing or achieving something more directly and quickly than by ordinary procedure (Webster's Third New International Dictionary). Diese Definition muß hier zugrundegelegt werden, um zu einer brauchbaren deutschen Lösung zu gelangen, da alle Übersetzungen mit *Abkürzung* oder *kurzem Weg* etc. unverständlich sind. Andere Varianten wären: und man macht sie nicht einfacher, . . ./man kann sie nicht schneller lösen, . . ./man kommt nicht schneller ans Ziel, . . .

[42] *oder:* Diese Erkenntnis
Allerdings geht dann das Wortspiel verloren, weshalb ich persönlich auf jeden Fall die Lösung mit Wissen vorziehe.

[43] „Erzieher“ ist hier nicht richtig, da er sich vor allem um die Bildung des Charakters bemüht. Nur der Pädagoge vermittelt Wissen, und der Text handelt ja eindeutig von Wissensvermittlung.

[44] *oder:* Niemand sollte verzichten müssen auf . . ./Niemandem sollte . . . vorenthalten werden.

Stichwortverzeichnis